THE YULETIDE BANDIT

Mike McIntyre

THE YULETIDE BANDIT

By Mike McIntyre

GREAT PLAINS
PUBLICATIONS

Great Plains Publications
420 – 70 Arthur Street
Winnipeg, MB R3B 1G7
www.greatplains.mb.ca

Great Plains Publications gratefully acknowledges the financial
support provided for its publishing program by the Government of
Canada through the Book Publishing Industry Development
Program (BPIDP); the Canada Council for the Arts; as well as the
Manitoba Department of Culture, Heritage and Tourism; and the
Manitoba Arts Council.

Design & Typography by Relish Design Studio Inc.
Printed in Canada by Kromar Printing

CANADIAN CATALOGUING IN PUBLICATION DATA

Main entry under title:
McIntyre, Mike
   The yuletide bandit : a seven-year search for a serial criminal /
Mike McIntyre.

Includes bibliographical references and index.
   ISBN 1-894283-47-3

1. Syrnyk, Michael.   2. Bank robberies—Manitoba—Winnipeg.
3. Thieves—Manitoba—Winnipeg—Biography.   I. Title

HV6665.C3M234 2004   364.15'52'09712743   C2004-904011-1

To Chassity, Parker and "Peanut".

ACKNOWLEDGEMENTS

I would like to thank all the people who directly assisted in this project. Michael Syrnyk, Brent and Sheri Syrnyk, Winnipeg Police Service, Stony Mountain penitentiary, Brian Bell, Mike Cook, Jeff Gindin, Karen Fulham, Nicholas Hirst, Jon Thordarson, Bruce Owen, Photographers of the *Winnipeg Free Press*, Samantha Moar and Kevin Webster. Special acknowledgement to my wife, Chassity, and our son, Parker for their unconditional love, support and patience; Nadia Moharib for her valuable time and wonderful way with words; And Gregg Shilliday, Cheryl Miki and Jewls Dengl for the trust, opportunity and long leash they have provided.

This book is based entirely on actual events.

All material is factual and has been derived from the following sources: Extensive interviews with Michael Syrnyk at Stony Mountain penitentiary in 2004; Official court records, including letters of support, victim impact statements and psychiatric evaluations tendered during sentencing; Interviews with members of Syrnyk's family; Partial 911 transcripts; Police statements and reports; Complete statements from victims and witnesses; Interviews with Winnipeg Police investigators; Transcripts of bail and sentencing proceedings; Interviews with Crown and defence lawyers; Personal experience and research on the case; And previous published reports.

CHAPTER 1

Beads of sweat dripped down Michael David Syrnyk's face as his running shoes pounded the pavement in rhythmic motion. His shaggy brown hair flopped in his eyes. Left, right, left, right, left, right. Syrnyk counted the paces in his head, trying not to let his heavy breathing throw him off. He wanted to make sure he wasn't slowing down.

Syrnyk had been running for at least an hour. Or maybe two? He didn't really care about the time. It was his energy level that mattered, and Syrnyk felt like there was still gas in his tank. He picked up the pace. Syrnyk's steps became louder, harder, faster. He started feeling a burn in his legs. It was muggy and dark, and the streets of St. James were relatively quiet on this late summer night. Just the way he liked it. Most would view this as exercise. For Syrnyk, it was survival.

He would be 26 years old in a few days, and Syrnyk felt physically stronger and healthier than ever. Many people who run regularly speak of a "runner's high", the onslaught of endorphins and an almost obsessive need to keep furthering one's goals, often to the brink of exhaustion. For Syrnyk, it was much more. He first felt the high when he was about 12, running as fast and as far as he could, not wanting to stop. Now, 14 years later, he actually felt guilty on days he didn't run. Syrnyk yearned for the challenge running presented, and loved pushing himself to new heights. In his teens, Syrnyk ran a handful of races at school track meets, but didn't like the idea of competing against others. So he began competing with himself.

For extra motivation, Syrnyk often leaned on Odin, his canine companion and devoted best friend. The pair was inseparable. Until they began running. It usually wasn't long before Odin, a little black terrier, was leading the way, enjoying his off-leash freedom and shooting back a few "Are YOU coming?" looks at his owner. Syrnyk would push himself harder because of Odin, who seemed to have no limits.

Syrnyk had been obsessed with his health for many years, always keeping in good shape but never thinking he was fit enough. So he would push on, raising the bar higher and setting goals which seemed unreachable, but never were. At times, he'd cut his food intake down to almost nothing. Other times, he would purge, then force himself to vomit. Syrnyk always managed to keep his weight steady around 170 pounds – barely enough to fill out his 5'9 frame. While most people would describe his stature as average, Syrnyk was convinced others saw him as weak and unworthy. That motivated him to the point of dangerous obsession.

The Yuletide Bandit

Syrnyk was experiencing a new high on this particular night, one that seemed to parallel running in many ways. In his own mind, he had emotionally pushed himself to the limit and succeeded. He had faced his fears and conquered. Syrnyk, the former choirboy, had just become a criminal.

The previous day – August 15, 1995

The lunch rush was nearly over inside the Bank of Montreal. As the clock neared 1 p.m., only a few customers remained inside the Marion Street branch, located just south of Winnipeg's downtown. People didn't seem in much of a hurry to get their business done today, their red, sweaty faces showing relief as they walked in to be greeted with a blast of air-conditioning. Maureen and Margaret were the only tellers working the floor but had managed to keep the wait to a minimum. Maureen, 26, was handling customer service issues while Margaret, 41, took care of withdrawals and deposits. They were a smooth, efficient team. As traffic inside the bank began to thin out, a strange sight caught Maureen's eye.

Near the teller counter, just beside a couple of waiting customers, stood a man wearing a woman's wig. It was auburn. Maureen did a double-take; the shoulder-length straight hair was so obviously fake that fear began creeping through her body. Just above the man's lip sat a moustache, similar in colour to the wig. Maureen had no doubt it was also fake. Sunglasses covered the man's eyes. He was holding a brown envelope in his hand, and Maureen thought she saw a bulge in his jacket.

Banking 101 tells you that someone walking into your branch wearing a disguise is never a good thing. Maureen knew they were in trouble. She quickly looked towards Margaret, who was tied up with a customer and hadn't seemed to notice the stranger standing near her. Maureen couldn't take her eyes off the man, who appeared calm as he stood, glancing at the few people around him. He had taken a service number and seemed to be waiting until his turn was called. She tried to study his facial features closer, trying to remember every detail in the event she had to describe him to police. Maureen's heart jumped when the man looked directly at her, as if he noticed how suspiciously she was staring at him. He immediately moved behind a display case, now partially out of Maureen's sight. Maureen knew she had to act fast.

"I have to get something," she nervously told her customer, whose back was turned to the man. Maureen quickly walked towards the vault, stopping briefly to motion to Margaret, who seemed to pick up on her concerns. Maureen didn't stop, heading directly for the vault to call police. Margaret looked at the man in the wig, who was walking towards them but then stopped abruptly, only to turn back towards the entrance of the bank. Suddenly, he was moving fast. She noticed the man was wearing some kind of earpiece. "Do you need any help?" Margaret asked nervously. The man ignored her, and was out the front door in seconds. Margaret studied the man as he turned east, glancing back over his shoulder as if to check whether someone was following him. He walked towards the rear parking lot, then broke into a full run and disappeared between two large buildings.

Police were in the area within five minutes, as suspicious calls at banks always receive the highest priority. With an average of 75 bank jobs a year in Winnipeg, there was no such thing as being over-cautious. Two general patrol officers took a brief drive around the neighbourhood, looking for the strange man as described by dispatch. No one jumped out at the pair, who continued on to the bank to speak with the two shaken tellers. Police learned a surveillance camera had snapped a picture of the mysterious cross-dresser. A city-wide message was broadcast over the police radio that a bank robbery may have just been thwarted.

• • • • • •

The veteran teller immediately sensed trouble when the stranger walked into the Assiniboine Credit Union just after 1:30 p.m. on August 15. Marilyn, 45, had never seen this man before in the members-only branch on St. Mary's Road. He stood in line, swaying back and forth on his feet as if impatient or nervous. He kept staring down at his moving shoes. Marilyn called the customer to her window, noticing his auburn wig and moustache as he approached. He silently passed her a large brown envelope, turning it so a card taped to the outside was exposed. There was a handwritten message attached. "I WANT $4,000 IN CASH."

Several other female tellers in the bank had noticed the man but weren't close enough to see what he was doing. Sherri looked over at Jennifer, mouthing the words "Do you know him?" Jennifer shook her head and Sherri mouthed, "We are being robbed". Another teller whispered, "That guy has a disguise on" to a co-worker. Jennifer quietly moved towards a phone and dialled 911 as Marilyn continued to deal with the man. "Don't press any alarms or hidden buttons, cause I'm hooked up to the police bands and you'll be sorry," he said in a strong voice. Marilyn noticed he was wearing an earpiece. Then she saw a second message written on the envelope. "I WILL MAKE A HECK OF A MESS."

Marilyn tried to remain calm, telling the man she didn't have $4,000 readily available. "Give me what you have," he said. Marilyn opened her cash drawer, emptying all the bills into his envelope. The total was $2,847. "Did you give me all the small bills?" the man asked in a firm, demanding voice. Marilyn nodded. The man grabbed the package, turned and walked towards the exit. A young woman who'd been cashing a cheque held open the door for the man, unaware a robbery had just occurred.

Several credit union employees rushed to the front window of the bank as the man hurried away. Jennifer started pounding on the glass, trying in vain to catch the attention of a middle-aged woman sitting at a picnic table across the street, right where the man was passing. She hoped the woman could keep a look out for where he was going. Police rushed to the scene, quickly linking this call to the one just 30 minutes earlier on nearby Marion Street. It appeared the bank robber was living by the motto "If at first you don't succeed, try, try again."

CHAPTER 2

November 1995

The past 12 weeks had been anxious ones, with Michael Syrnyk constantly checking over his shoulder, certain the police were going to come calling. But they hadn't. Syrnyk had been very careful inside the two banks and clearly hadn't left much behind for police to work with. It had been close, especially his first failed attempt when he heard the alarm call come over the police scanner which he had stuffed inside his jacket attached to an earpiece he was wearing. Without the scanner, he likely would have been caught on the spot, unaware one of the clerks had managed to call for help while he foolishly stood in line looking like a stereotypical example of guy about to rob a bank. He realized now what a terrible disguise it had been and how obvious he must have looked. Thankfully, the mistake hadn't come back to haunt him.

• • • • • •

The idea to become a criminal surfaced about a year earlier in the back room of the family butcher shop. Syrnyk was working with his dad cutting meat. He felt most comfortable in the back room; away from the customers he struggled to serve during eight-hour shifts which always seemed much longer. He would develop headaches, anxiety and panic attacks – not unlike the feeling described by people who suffer heart attacks. Tingling arms. Chest pains. Profuse sweating. Blurred vision. Even incidental contact with people would set Syrnyk's heart racing. He had trouble making eye contact. When people around him would laugh Syrnyk assumed he was the butt of their jokes. He regularly told himself people hated him. But he never knew why.

Syrnyk usually went straight home from work and grabbed his dog, Odin. They would go for long walks and runs, often for hours at a time. It was the highlight of Syrnyk's day. Syrnyk always hoped to clear his head during these private times with Odin but usually returned home more confused and worried about the world than ever.

One morning, Syrnyk awoke to his alarm clock and needed every ounce of strength he had to get up out of bed. "Fuck!" He slammed his fist down on the clock. Life had never seemed less pointless. After more than three long years at the shop, Syrnyk was ready to quit – even if it meant incurring the wrath of his father. He slowly lumbered into work, taking the usual spot behind the counter that quickly lined up with customers. A nervous Syrnyk went through the paces, the clock seeming to move slower than ever. Lunchtime finally arrived. Syrnyk retreated to the backroom and began leafing through a newspaper sitting on the table. A small story on one of the back pages caught his eye. A daring heist had occurred the day before in Ontario. Two masked, armed men pounced on an armoured car guard, assaulted him and then walked away with a bag full of money. Police and witnesses described the men as extremely calm and obviously prepared. They had made off with nearly $250,000. A light bulb went on in Syrnyk's head that day. It wasn't long before he told his dad he was quitting. To hell with what the old man thought.

• • • • • •

The plan was to start small. Syrnyk picked the early morning hours of August 20, 1994 to test the waters, finally winning a tug-of-war with his conscience. Syrnyk convinced himself he *needed* to do this. There were no other options. The days of honesty were over. His fate was sealed.

Like every tradesperson, a good criminal needs quality tools. Syrnyk knew the S.I.R. outdoor supply store on Ellice Avenue was a great place to load up. Armed with a drill and chop saw, he went to the Winnipeg gun shop just after 3 a.m.. He wore rubber gloves on his hands, careful not to leave fingerprints behind. Syrnyk went to the back of the store, wanting to be protected from any vehicular traffic that happened to pass by. The door had two steel deadbolts that Syrnyk immediately went to work on by drilling through the keyholes. He sawed through the lower bolt and gained entry to the store in no time. Syrnyk was greeted by the shrill sound of an alarm. He jumped in surprise.

Syrnyk worked fast, heading straight to the glass display cases housing the weaponry. He smashed through it quickly and grabbed whatever he could, knowing there wasn't time to waste. There were a few neat toys, including five sets of binoculars, two night vision scopes and two handheld global positioning units. Syrnyk took some serious artillery in the form of 14 handguns of just about every make. Glocks, Smith and Wessons, Rugers. Syrnyk also stole three shotguns and a Chinese assault rifle that appeared to be antique. He fled the building with the alarm still blaring, thankful to find the back of the store still clear of any cars or people. Syrnyk escaped safely before police arrived.

What had he done? Syrnyk's conscience wasn't done fighting and took a serious round out of him in the weeks following the heist. Plagued with guilt and remorse, Syrnyk began disposing of several guns by dumping them into the Assiniboine River near the St. James home where he was living.

• • • • • •

Elementary school at Lord Roberts was so "normal" that Syrnyk now looked back and wondered whether he was even the same person. He actually had a few young friends and always seemed to be able to make other kids laugh. Not bust a gut type laughing, but enough to know he was appreciated. Syrnyk would do goofy things, just making faces or voices that always seemed to get a response. He remembered going to childhood birthday parties, getting laughs from other children by acting like he had a disability or talking in a stupid voice. It was lowbrow humour, but they were all young and silly so it didn't seem to matter.

The first sign of trouble came around age 14 when Syrnyk began having unusual fantasies. He dreamed about becoming a cocaine smuggler, like the people he heard about on television or read about in the newspapers and magazines he would read cover-to-cover. But he wouldn't be an ordinary drug mule. No, Syrnyk wanted to ply his trade in a submarine. He would build it with his own hands. Never mind that Winnipeg was smack dab in the middle of the country making drug trafficking by boat or submarine a somewhat far-fetched plan. Syrnyk thought he could find a way to make it work. He also dreamed of becoming a safecracker, which would test both his brainpower and willpower and allow him to work alone. What exciting work it would be!

Syrnyk had never seen a psychiatrist but he considered himself somewhat of an expert in the field. He had read numerous pamphlets and brochures on schizophrenia, bi-polar disorder and other mental ailments and often felt like he was reading a synopsis of his life. At bare minimum, Syrnyk believed he was manic-depressive. How else to explain the wild mood swings which had bothered him since his early teens. At age 15, Syrnyk had frozen as he tried to board a crowded transit bus. He couldn't make the short walk up the stairs, drop his coins in the till and take a seat. He hated the thought of being confined in a small space with so many people. The bus incident marked a major turning point in Syrnyk's life.

He was also becoming increasingly obsessed about his health as he got older, believing death was just waiting around the corner to take him. He was convinced he had cancer by age 15. The glands in his neck felt lumpy and Syrnyk figured they must be tumours. He kept his worries private, never sharing them with his family or any doctor. He suffered in silence. Cleanliness was another obsession and Syrnyk went to absurd lengths to put his mind at ease. There were times as a child when he used a razor blade to scrape skin off his hands, believing it was the only way to get them clean. This painful procedure would be repeated for years. Syrnyk would wash his hands dozens of times in a day, rubbing them raw and leaving them red and wrinkled. His room was always tidy and organized. But sometimes, it would start spinning. Paranoid thoughts would consume his mind, leaving Syrnyk to believe people wanted to hurt him. He often thought about his own initials, and came up with his own personal meaning – M.D.S. stood for Manic Depressed Sociopath.

The Yuletide Bandit

Junior high school at Churchill High was an emotional roller coaster. An eager, fresh-faced Syrnyk gave way to the troubled teen that would isolate himself from his peers. He became his own entity; a one-man crew that nobody seemed to be able to figure out and everyone was content to just leave alone. Most people thought Syrnyk was a nice guy who was just shy, a bit of a loner who always seemed to do well on tests. Teachers loved him because he was a model student in many ways, doing good work and causing no problems in the classroom. Syrnyk never had problems with his classmates and this peace and tranquillity he imposed on himself spared him some of the typical teen trauma he watched others go through. He always believed kids who tried too hard to fit in were just asking to be picked on. Some did try to befriend Syrnyk, but he wasn't interested and simply brushed them off. Syrnyk worried about offending people, believing he would open his mouth and say the wrong thing. He was meek, usually speaking in a quiet, emotionless voice that people strained to hear. He found himself second-guessing the occasional routine, mundane conversations he would have with classmates.

Syrnyk would lay awake at night replaying things he said and get angry with himself, thinking he'd come across like a fool. He also worried kids would hurt his feelings, so his solution was to avoid conversations with others at all costs. Syrnyk had trouble trusting anyone, believing they must have an ulterior motive for wanting to be his friend. How could somebody want to be friends with someone like him? What did he have to offer? Syrnyk regularly asked himself these questions and never could provide answers. The result was a self-imposed loneliness that haunted him into adulthood.

Syrnyk never played organized team sports because he didn't see himself as a team player. A couple girls, pretty and relatively popular, had asked Syrnyk to go see a movie in his teen years. He declined. He feared he was being set up for some cruel joke or that the girls were simply taking pity on him. Besides, he never felt like he would know what to say or how to act in their company. Simply cutting himself off was the easiest solution.

Syrnyk had a spotless youth record, easily resisting any temptation to get involved in trouble. He never smoked cigarettes or did drugs and was brutally honest. At 16, Syrnyk was standing inside a 7-Eleven store browsing through magazines when he saw a wallet lying on the floor. He rushed over, picked it up and could feel it was thick with bills. He had no hesitation in bringing it to the store clerk and turning it in, not even pausing to open it for a curious glance. It's not like he really wanted the money – Syrnyk never considered himself materialistic. His tastes in clothes were basic – jeans and t-shirts. If he needed new clothes, a trip to the nearest thrift store or Salvation Army would do the trick. He never worried about keeping up with the latest fashions, or whether he had the hippest brand names. It all seemed so artificial, and Syrnyk couldn't stand the thought of being a walking billboard.

High school was a personal hell for Syrnyk. His inner turmoil was much worse and caused his grades to tank but a natural intellect stopped a "C" from becoming an "F". He would often skip classes, but not to go hang out at the mall or the movie theatres. Instead, he would take long walks or runs. It was all part of wanting to be in his own world, free of the complications and burdens that come with relationships and responsibilities to others. Syrnyk wanted to like school but found he was no longer being challenged. His mind would drift during class and a need to be isolated in his own world consumed him.

He never fit in, not that he ever made much of an effort. Virginia and Mike Syrnyk Sr. didn't say much about Syrnyk's faltering grades, content to leave him be just so long as he passed. And he did, graduating from Churchill High School in 1989. Not surprisingly, Syrnyk didn't go to his grad party.

Religion and spirituality were constant sources of inner-debate with Syrnyk, who would argue with himself about the role they played in his life and society as a whole. His parents never went to church, but Syrnyk and his brother, Brent, were sent to a Winnipeg parish for a couple of years while both boys were still in elementary school. A big bus would come by their home Sunday mornings – Syrnyk and Brent called it "The Joy Bus" – and they would board along with several neighbourhood children. Most kids shuddered at the sight of the bus with the big crosses painted on the sides. But unlike the others, Syrnyk actually enjoyed going to Sunday School services, where he would listen intently and give deep thought to what was being said. He wanted to believe in God and Syrnyk definitely felt like there was a higher power controlling everyone's fate. But he remained as confused at age 25 as he did at age 10, searching for proof of God's existence but not finding anything that satisfied him.

John Milton bestowed his great masterpiece upon the world in 1667. It arrived in Syrnyk's hands some 325 years later. According to Milton, his collection of books titled *Paradise Lost* were about "man's disobedience and the loss thereupon of Paradise wherein he was placed; the prime cause of his fall, the serpent, or rather Satan the serpent, who, revolting from God and drawing to his side many legions of angels, was by command of God driven out of heaven with all his crew into the great deep." Syrnyk felt a deep, spiritual attraction to Milton's work, one that led him to read *Paradise Lost* too many times to count. Essentially, it was the ultimate battle of good versus evil. Syrnyk found himself often questioning which side of that battle he was on.

Syrnyk began escaping reality through movies, but hardly the pop-culture fluff that seems to drive most teens. He first saw *Clockwork Orange* in his mid-teens and immersed himself into moviemaker Stanley Kubric's messed-up world of futuristic London, where criminals run rampant on the streets. The main character, Alex, is a bright but extremely violent and sadistic teen gang leader who, along with his fellow gang members called the Droogs, roam the city at night in search of victims to terrorize. Their crimes include random beatings, robbery and rape. Alex narrates the story, referring to their practices as "ultra violence". His fellow gangsters begin to question Alex's authority and set him up to be caught in the act by police. Alex is eventually convicted and sentenced to prison, where he learns of an experimental psychological treatment being sanctioned by the government that guarantees an early release from prison. Alex – the government guinea pig – is supposedly "cured" by the treatment and released back on the streets. In essence, he no longer controls his own mind and the people he has harmed return to seek revenge. Syrnyk found the groundbreaking, 1971 movie overwhelming at times but would watch it repeatedly, seeming to learn something new each time. The violence was brutal, almost unbearable. And while he sometimes would abruptly shut the VCR off, it wasn't long before it was back on. Syrnyk was fascinated with Alex. He wished he could trade places with him in life, to have his power and find his own group of Droogs to lead. Alex didn't control his own mind. And Syrnyk felt his was slowly slipping away as well.

Apocalypse Now and *The Grapes of Wrath* were two other favourites. Syrnyk would morph himself into the various characters, often wishing he could escape his own tortured world and join theirs. How neat it would be to become a rebel soldier devoid of thoughts and emotions. Syrnyk had no time for comic books, entertainment magazines, video games or computers. Instead, he would bury himself in magazines such as *Soldier of Fortune*, a pro-military, pro-American journal that believes everyone has a right to bear arms. *S.W.A.T.* was another favourite, filled with insightful news on the latest in weapons, tactics and training. Syrnyk had no desire to join the military but was fascinated to read about the world outside his locked bedroom door. He also enjoyed the sanctity and peacefulness of libraries and was excited by the seemingly never-ending wealth of material they had to offer. He tried to absorb as much information as possible, often spending full days at a desk, a large pile of books spread out in front of him.

Straight out of high school, Syrnyk was at a crossroads. With the urging of his parents he enrolled in criminology at the University of Winnipeg, not really knowing why. As a small child he had thought about becoming a police officer or fire fighter, probably not unlike most kids his age. But it was no longer something he desired. Syrnyk dropped out of university after only a few weeks. The people were getting to him, the classes much bigger than high school. He couldn't concentrate, and wasn't enjoying it. He felt paralyzed with fear. So he quit and began working for his dad at the butcher shop.

Syrnyk's first sexual experience came at age 19. It was money well spent. Who knew what her name was? There had been so many others since that it all seemed somewhat blurry. It was part of the deep loneliness Syrnyk felt, an inability to connect with others on what shrinks would likely call a normal human level. So he found comfort in the arms of prostitutes, women who would treat him like the most important man in the world for 10 minutes, half an hour, or however long he was paying for. Then he'd walk away. No commitment, no attachment, no problem. There were times, when the depression would seem to be out of control, that Syrnyk felt disgusted with himself. He knew what he was doing was pathetic. But Syrnyk grew to like bought sex. He felt a type of high, not unlike running. It was a matter of power and control. Syrnyk knew Winnipeg's massage parlours inside out and there were very few where the only thing on the menu was truly just a back-rub. For the right price a man could have just about anything he wanted. The frequency of Syrnyk's visits depended on his mood. There were weeks he'd go three times, and other times he'd stay away for months.

With no social life to speak of, Syrnyk managed to save some money. He cashed it in during his early 20s when the criminal lifestyle began to appeal to him. Syrnyk read on the back of *Soldier of Fortune* about an American company called Palladin Press which specialized in how-to manuals for making silencers, detonating bombs with cellular phones and stealing cars. He took out about $1,000 from his bank account and ordered nearly every book they had.

Syrnyk was worried the books would draw suspicion from overzealous Customs officials if he tried to have them sent into Canada. So he sent a cheque by mail and put a return address for a postal box in the American border town of Walhalla, North Dakota, just over an hour south of Winnipeg. He cleverly devised a plan to drive near the border late one night, park his car near a field on the Manitoba side and walk across into the U.S. without being detected. He hiked at least 15 miles that night, both ways, through the bush. The books weighed 50 pounds, so the return trip was even harder. But Syrnyk persevered, anxious to return to Winnipeg to begin reading. He had a lot to learn. Syrnyk also began watching as many true crime programs as possible, shows like *Unsolved Mysteries* and *City Confidential*. He had always been a good student and now he was becoming a student of crime.

• • • • • •

November 15, 1995

Winter was about to start placing its grip on Winnipeg, but a little cold air wouldn't keep Syrnyk inside. He was out for one of his regular strolls in a residential area near his home and was seriously considering doing a break-and-enter as a means to further challenge himself and his criminal desires. It certainly wasn't about stealing someone else's property. Syrnyk was dressed in black, carrying a dark backpack. Inside was a semi-automatic replica pistol loaded with several rounds of blank ammunition. He also had some common tools and a canister of pepper spray, in case he found himself in any trouble.

By mid-evening, Syrnyk saw a home that appeared to be empty and approached it, crouching down in the front yard to get a better look. Suddenly, a police car pulled up behind with their lights shining directly on him. Syrnyk was frozen with fear. He couldn't move. Two uniformed officers got out, holding their flashlights and quickly walked over. "What's your name?" the officer asked sternly. Syrnyk panicked, refusing to give his name. He didn't know what to say or how to act. Police grabbed his backpack and opened it up. They began searching the contents, pulling out the tools, the pepper spray and the semi-automatic pistol. Syrnyk was ordered to turn around with his hands behind his back. "You're under arrest. You have the right to remain silent…"

CHAPTER 3

Michael Syrnyk dodged a bullet. His arrest had led to charge of trespassing and possessing break-in tools but nothing more serious. Fortunately for him, Winnipeg police had no way of linking him to the pair of bank jobs or the weapons haul. The officers questioned Syrnyk about other unsolved break-ins, figuring he was a bit of a specialist given the tools he was carrying at the time. Syrnyk said very little to the officers the night of his arrest, at first even refusing to give his name. The police identified him as "John Doe". Syrnyk eventually settled down and gave them his identity, satisfied they didn't know anything more about his recent criminal background and that it was best to not cause any additional trouble for himself. Sure enough, he was on his way in a matter of hours, spending a few hours in the Winnipeg Remand Centre until being released on bail. Before he left, police took Syrnyk's fingerprints. This was not the ideal situation for a man who had some big plans. But it could have been much worse. Syrnyk knew he would have to be more careful if he wanted to succeed as a criminal.

July 1996

The anxious days and sleepless nights were taking a toll on Syrnyk, whose fragile mind was proving to be his own worst enemy. He figured it was just a matter of time before the police showed up at his door, arrest warrant in hand, ready to lock him up for much more then just a few hours. The fear of getting caught by police was never-ending and Syrnyk decided to take drastic action. Under the cover of darkness, he made another trip to the river and gave some more of his arsenal a watery burial.

Syrnyk realized now, eight months after his initial arrest, that the brush with police had shaken his already fragile confidence to the core. He dealt with his criminal charges by pleading guilty and walked out of court moments later with a small fine and a criminal record. With the court case behind him, Syrnyk felt it was time to get out of Winnipeg. It would be easier to clear his head and get re-focused. Syrnyk said a few quick good-byes to his family, and then boarded a Greyhound bus with a one-way ticket to Calgary.

● ● ● ● ● ●

Virgina Alice Jones, daughter of David Jones and Doris Kalika, was four months pregnant when she walked down the aisle and married Mike Joseph Peter Syrnyk on March 1, 1969 in Winnipeg. She was 24 and a lifetime resident of Winnipeg. He was 22, originally from Moncton, New Brunswick. The blushing bride gave birth to their son, Michael David, on August 26. Exactly one year later, Virginia was pregnant with their second child. Brent Stephen was born May 20, 1971. The early years were stressful, as money was tight and tempers would often flare. Alcohol was usually at the centre of the problems. With the two boys in school, Virginia went to work as a receptionist at the Assiniboine Credit Union in downtown Winnipeg making $375 a week before taxes. Mike Sr. was working as a butcher and meat manager making $500 per week. Life only got harder for the Syrnyk family as the children grew up. "Why don't you guys just get a divorce?" an angry Brent and Michael would often tell their parents, who seemed more intent on fighting with each other then looking after the kids' needs. "You don't even treat each other like humans." Syrnyk was especially disgusted at the way his parents treated each other, but kept his emotions inside for fear of angering his father or hurting his mother.

Virginia and Mike Sr.'s marriage reached a breaking point in 1989 following years of arguments and even violence. On October 25, Virginia called the police on her husband, reporting she had been assaulted. Mike Sr. was charged, and released on bail with conditions to have no contact with his wife. Virginia and her two sons, now in their late teens, continued to live together at the family's modest home on Blackwater Bay in Winnipeg. Mike Sr. went to stay with a friend in St. James.

On November 6, 1989, Virginia filed for divorce and a restraining order preventing her husband from having any contact with her. She painted an ugly picture of their 20-year marriage in a series of affidavits. "The marriage between myself and the respondent has been a difficult one. The respondent, when he drinks, tends to be violent towards myself and has assaulted me frequently since the beginning of our marriage. I stayed with the respondent to ensure that my children had a good home and in the hope that he would reform his ways," she wrote. Virginia said she was afraid of her husband, especially when he gets drunk. "The numerous assaults which have taken place have been occasioned by the respondent getting drunk. After several of these assaults in the past I have had to see my doctor who has noted the bruises I received." Virginia claimed she was swimming in debt – although she had racked up the expenses in recent months as her marriage deteriorated. Credit cards were stretched to the limit. Visa carried a $2,400 debt. A Petro Canada card had a $500 balance. Virginia owed more than $1,000 to Eaton's and The Bay. And she still owed $8,000 on a bank loan.

Virginia's affidavit sparked an angry response by Mike Sr. on November 20. "The petitioner is correct in stating that the marriage has been a difficult one. For the last 10 years, the marriage has not been happy for either my spouse or myself. In retrospect, a separation should have occurred long ago and in fairness, it is probably correct that we stayed together for the kids' sake and for our own financial security only," he began. "Your deponent acknowledges some violence existed, but the petitioner is not being forthright in attributing sole blame for such violence to me. In fact, neither the petitioner nor your deponent are what I would consider to be alcoholics, however, we both on occasion, drink to excess. During such times, fights have erupted which did involve some shoving back and forth, however, your deponent has never punched the petitioner during the course of our marriage." Mike Sr. said he "was not proud" of the violence which existed but claimed it was always a result of "antagonistic" behaviour from his wife. "Your deponent has had cold water thrown on him, while he slept in bed. He has had his covers pulled off him while sleeping in bed. On many occasions, he has had his shirts ripped and buttons torn off his clothing," the affidavit stated. Mike Sr. claimed problems in the family, such as when Brent or Michael would skip school in years past or when an evening out together involved another woman talking to him, Virginia would lash out with violence. He said he stopped sleeping in the same bedroom as his wife weeks earlier, which led to continuous arguments. Mike Sr. accused his wife of going to a party on October 23, getting drunk, passing out and not returning home until two days later. He began moving all his items downstairs on October 25, and Virginia got upset because he had taken a quilt she claimed was hers. Another argument broke out over his use of a radio. Mike Sr. claimed a shoving match ensued, which was broken up 18-year-old Brent. In his counter-affidavit, he also took issue with many of the financial figures his wife used, claiming she was exaggerating their monthly expenses.

Round Two began on November 28 with another affidavit from Virginia. "The respondents affidavit does not accurately set forth the degree or nature of the violence which the respondent inflicted on me. Our fights did not just involve shoving…but were very violent at times. Many of the incidents of violence took place in front of our children throughout the years and they would certainly be able to attest to the degree and nature of violence," she wrote. Mike Sr. fired back, denying that either Brent or Michael were witness to any violence in the home. "This is clearly not the case and, furthermore, I am aware of the fact that the children do not wish to become involved in this dispute for either the benefit of myself or my wife," he said.

And so it went, back and forth, on and on until January 22, 1990. The ugly legal battle was taking a financial toll on both Virginia and Mike Sr. and the game of domestic "chicken" ended when Virginia was the first to get out of the way. "The petitioner, Virginia Alice Syrnyk, wholly discontinues this action against the respondent, Michael Joseph Peter Syrnyk," read a one-page document filed in Court of Queen's Bench. Just like that. Although their problems certainly weren't over, Virginia and Mike Sr. decided to take their fight out of the courtroom and back into the home where it had been for 20 years. It would be cheaper that way – although the cost to their children had yet to fully be measured.

•••••••

The image was burned in his mind; a permanent souvenir of Calgary he wished didn't exist. The bank teller, a pretty young woman, overcome with fear as Syrnyk handed her a note demanding money. He had never seen someone cry like that before, a never-ending steam of tears flowing from her wide eyes. An older lady had taken over for the frightened girl, stuffing the envelope with money while giving Syrnyk a look that seemed to be saying "You bastard. Look what you've done." Syrnyk had tried to wipe away this memory, to forget her face. He couldn't.

Syrnyk actually did two hold-ups while in Calgary on the same day and both went off without any glitches. He didn't even bother with a goofy disguise, content just to put some sunglasses over his hazel eyes and a baseball cap to hide his shaggy hair. No women's wigs or moustaches this time. There were two clean getaways, no obvious evidence left behind and a nice wad of spending cash. Of course, Syrnyk didn't really need a lot of money, as he was staying in a relatively cheap hotel, only venturing out occasionally to hit a massage parlour or to peak inside a gun store. Syrnyk knew he would have to re-load soon.

Syrnyk's return to Winnipeg hadn't been the homecoming he was hoping for. His parents were fighting worse then ever and again living apart, this time for good. Brent was living alone in an apartment and Syrnyk split his time between Brent and his mother. He avoided his father as much as possible. The tension in the family was thick.

Brent was the one person Syrnyk felt he could really trust, but still had difficulty opening up. In the fall of 1997, Syrnyk's rage was ready to explode.

• • • • • •

September 10, 1997

Winnipeg police were called to a disturbance inside a home on College Avenue, located in the city's North End, just before midnight. Two uniformed officers went inside the residence, leaving their cruiser car parked on the street just outside the neighbouring home. As they stood inside taking statements from the occupants, four loud blasts filled the air. The sound of shattering glass followed. Police immediately recognized the sounds as coming from a shotgun and drew their own weapons. They carefully crept outside the home, scanning the scene for the source of the blasts. Nothing was seen. Police radioed in a call for immediate backup, saying shots had just been fired in the area. Several cars quickly swarmed the neighbourhood. Police noticed nine holes in the driver's side door of the police cruiser. Three spent, 12-gauge shotguns shells lay in the nearby grass. Police found another seven holes in the front vinyl siding of the home they'd been standing inside of, including two pellets that had penetrated the triple pane living room window. Sixteen pellets had struck the front concrete steps, while two others were lodged inside a flowerpot on the top step. A total of 36 pellets were recovered, consistent with four rounds being fired. What the hell had just happened?

Syrnyk sprinted into the darkness still clutching his shotgun, headed towards his waiting car. The four shots had been perfect but his anger still hadn't subsided. God help whoever crossed his path tonight. Syrnyk continued driving, being careful as always to use his traffic signals and keep his speed down, for fear of attracting attention and being pulled over. He didn't have a clear game plan, but knew he wasn't finished. There was too much rage. As the clock passed midnight, Syrnyk saw a police station in the distance. It was the District 6 headquarters on Pembina Highway, in the south end of the city. An empty, full marked Ford Explorer was sitting outside the police station. It was a supervisor's vehicle. This was too tempting. Syrnyk parked his car, walked a short distance and stopped. He raised the shotgun, taking aim at the Explorer. Syrnyk squeezed the trigger 12 times, each blast releasing a myriad of pent-up emotions. He pictured his parents – especially his father – each time he fired the gun. Syrnyk sprayed the driver's side rear doors and the bumper, blowing out several windows. He calmly turned around, got into his car and drove away.

CHAPTER 4

Winnipeg police had a loose cannon on their hands. The seemingly unprovoked shooting of two cruiser cars, located halfway across the city from each other and separated by less than an hour, was cause for major alarm and even panic. A police car being spat on, kicked or even keyed was a semi-regular occurrence in Winnipeg, especially in some of the higher crime areas. After all, there were enough people with disrespect for authority that – fuelled by a little liquid courage – wouldn't hesitate to leave their mark in a relatively harmless way. But riddling a police car with bullets was not only rare, it was frightening. Police had enough to deal with without worrying that a gun-toting psychopath was on the prowl. Had there only been the first shooting in the North End the concern wouldn't have been as great. Perhaps then it had just been the work of a drunk wanting to impress his liquored-up friends or even a street gang initiation. But the fact the gunman took the time to drive to the other end of the city, then take aim at a car sitting directly outside a packed police station suggested a more chilling motive. It was clearly pre-meditated.

Police had little evidence to work with, and even less idea about the gunman's intentions. Would his next target be an actual officer?

● ● ● ● ● ●

January 1, 1998

As Winnipeggers were ringing in the New Year at house parties, bars and social halls, Michael Syrnyk was quietly embarking on his own private celebration. 1998 was going to be a big year and Syrnyk knew his first step was to re-load. He had four banks under his belt, but hadn't done one in the city for more than two years. That was about to change. Syrnyk's personal and family life was in shambles; his parents still at each other's throats and feelings of depression, anxiety and even suicide filled his mind daily. Syrnyk had blown off some steam in September, shooting up the cop cars in a hair-trigger response to the ongoing frustrations with his family. He didn't want to confront his father so he decided to dish out his anger on another form of authority in the police. Syrnyk knew the incident had caught the attention of police and deliberately kept a low profile in the subsequent weeks. Now it was time to get back into the game.

In the early morning hours of New Year's Day, Syrnyk turned his stolen car towards the Wal-Mart store on St. Mary's Road located in the south end of Winnipeg. A shotgun lay beside him, one of the few weapons he hadn't dumped into the river yet. Syrnyk pulled into the parking lot, which was empty of cars but filled with several large snow piles. He headed for the east side of the store because it was most sheltered from passing traffic. Syrnyk used his shotgun to smash the glass from the doors, reaching his hand through the broken shards to open the latch. The move immediately triggered an alarm. Syrnyk was wearing his police scanner and earpiece so he could hear when the call was broadcast to police. He knew he'd have to work quickly but was counting on police being relatively busy with rowdy New Year's revelers. Syrnyk went straight for the back of Wal-Mart, towards the glass display case housing the weapons. He had previously come to the store on a scouting mission and knew exactly where to go. He raised his shotgun and squeezed the trigger, blowing out the sliding glass door. The shot actually struck the stock of a rifle sitting upright in the case. Syrnyk began emptying the contents, grabbing six 12-gauge shotguns and dumping them into a bag. A Remington Viper .22 calibre rifle also caught his eye and Syrnyk added it to the pile. He turned around to leave just as the alarm call was being broadcast to the units in the area. Syrnyk ran to his car, making a clean getaway moments before the first patrol car arrived on scene. The New Year was off to a good start.

Police had very little to work with. No fingerprints, no traceable footprints. Tire tracks seemed to indicate the culprit had fled in a vehicle.

The theft of weapons was always a major concern, as the items probably weren't headed for safekeeping in someone's harmless gun collection. Police planned to speak with the usual suspects and contact their various street sources fishing for information about the stolen haul. It was unlikely the sudden availability of half-a-dozen guns could stay a secret for very long. Firearms were usually sold quickly on the streets, or altered by criminals who would saw off part of the barrel so the weapon was more compact and more dangerous.

• • • • • •

January 8, 1998

"Give me the money. Just give me everything and nobody will get hurt!" Syrnyk screamed at the frightened, 22-year-old female teller, holding an open white pillowcase in one gloved hand. A 12-gauge shotgun was in his other hand. Today marked a new beginning for Syrnyk, who had resolved to use a more aggressive, in-your-face approach. It was the first time he had gone into a bank with a weapon, although he had kept the chamber empty just to be safe. The six employees inside the Crosstown Credit Union in the northern part of Winnipeg didn't know the difference. Syrnyk picked this Henderson Highway location in north Winnipeg because he liked the security a back lane provided to leave his waiting getaway car. He had spent the first few days of the New Year driving around the city, looking for his next target.

The Yuletide Bandit

Syrnyk burst in through the main doors of the normally busy branch just after 9 a.m., ignoring the fact several customers were also inside at the time. One of those customers was a 77-year-old man. Syrnyk went directly behind the front counter to confront the female tellers. A white mask covered his face with only the eyeholes cut out. The first young woman he encountered was shaking. "Get it in, get it in!" he shouted, holding open the pillowcase. Syrnyk lowered his shotgun to waist level, not pointing it directly at the woman. She complied with his demands for money, putting small bills like fives and tens inside the pillowcase. He quickly grew impatient and reached his hand into her till, grabbing a wad of twenties, fifties and hundred dollar bills. Syrnyk had put a bent clothes hanger inside the mouth of the pillowcase so it would stay open, a clever trick he'd read in one of his how-to books. He then attached the makeshift bag to the cylinder of his shotgun with a string, just to make it easier to hold them both and still have a hand free.

He was also wearing three different layers of clothes so he could shed them as he made good on his escape to ensure nobody got an accurate description of him. Syrnyk walked over to a pair of other tellers – older women who seemed more relaxed. They also filled his bag with bills. Syrnyk was listening for the police call but nothing had come over the scanner yet. Still, he kept a quick pace, but stumbled as he tried to flee. The gate wouldn't open, leaving him temporarily stuck behind the counter. He scurried to the other side, this time opening the gate. As Syrnyk neared the exit he turned towards the shocked customers and staff. "Thank you. Now nobody move and nobody will get hurt," he said. With that parting politeness, Syrnyk was out the door within 90 seconds of first entering the bank.

Winnipeg police units rushed to the scene as the call for a robbery went out over the airwaves at 9:11 a.m.. Officers were split up, with some going directly to the scene and others conducting a search of the immediate area. The only suspect description was a masked man with a shotgun or rifle, believed to be fleeing westbound on Hawthorne Avenue. Two general patrol constables began searching on foot, meeting up with the canine team. The police dog, named Joker, quickly picked up a human scent despite the fresh dump of snow from overnight. The track went west on Hawthorne, turning north on Henderson Highway. Police had their guns drawn preparing for a possible confrontation with an armed fugitive.

As the search went down Henderson the officers spotted something up ahead. Two shotgun shells, red in colour, were sticking out of the white snow. A third shell was found nearby. Police continued the track for another block, until Joker came to an abrupt halt. Tire tracks and what appeared to be a piece of the curb broken off told the unfortunate story. The bandit had likely driven away from the scene. He had obviously been in a hurry, hitting the curb in the process.

Identification officers came to the scene but were unable to take any suitable footprint impressions from the snow. The shotgun shells were bagged but would provide little information to investigators because there were no fingerprints. The news got worse – a video surveillance camera inside the credit union had briefly stopped working while the tape rewound just as the robbery was occurring. Police were frustrated, telling the bank manager to rewind the tape next time before they open for business. Witnesses also gave varying descriptions of the culprit that only added to the confusion. Some described the man as being in his late thirties, about 5'10, 180 pounds. Others pegged him as being in his late teens or early twenties, perhaps 5'5 with a slim build. These were not the types of descriptions from which composite sketches could be made.

● ● ● ● ● ●

January 12, 1998

Syrnyk had made off with $5,389. His first Winnipeg robbery in more than two years – and his fifth overall – had been the most successful one yet. He was really starting to get the feel for this, brimming with confidence and feeling much better about himself, and his life. Syrnyk didn't want to let this feeling go. So, four days later, he headed towards the Toronto-Dominion Bank on St. Mary's Road. There would be no rest for the wicked.

"Move over! Give me your money!" Syrnyk leaped over the counter, landing on his feet and startling everyone inside the bank just after 10 a.m.. He wasn't going to waste time with the gate. Clad behind a white ski mask, he reached into his pillowcase and pulled out the sawed off shotgun. This time the gun was loaded – with rock salt. Syrnyk wanted to ensure there wouldn't be any damage if the gun accidentally fired. There were audible screams and gasps from staff and a handful of customers. Syrnyk could see fear in their eyes, although he took no extra joy in that. An older man, appearing to be the manager, tried to keep his staff calm by assuring them everything would be okay. The teller, a middle-aged man, didn't waste any time opening the till. Syrnyk was pressing the shotgun against the man's side, the first time he'd actually put his weapon directly against a victim's body. Syrnyk grabbed the money himself, worried that the employee would slip in an exploding dye-pack if he let him do it. He knew this was a popular ploy by banks to mark criminals for future identification. Syrnyk fled the bank quickly, turning east and running towards his stolen car parked in a nearby lane. He was $3,100 richer.

Also for the first time, Syrnyk had set up two cars – the initial getaway vehicle, and then a second one a few miles away. He was becoming a pro at stealing cars, largely favouring the heavily populated River Heights neighbourhood in Winnipeg because it was close to home and the supply seemed endless. Tall trees and bushy shrubs in the area also provided a good cover, especially at night. Syrnyk had researched the art of car theft well, and it was paying dividends. He felt it would be easier to keep police guessing if he didn't stay with one car. He also made sure to rip off his outer layer of clothing as he fled. Syrnyk was only four blocks away when he saw two police cars coming towards him, their lights flashing and sirens blaring. He panicked – but calmed down as the cruisers kept driving straight past him and towards the bank he'd just robbed.

A Nike shoe. Police could put a brand name to their suspect, thanks to a series of clear prints he'd left in the snow and the wonders of modern science. The impressions measured 31 centimetres by 10 centimetres, indicating a man of average size. They matched the same dirty shoeprints the masked bandit had left on a black desk blotter when he jumped over the counter inside the bank. Considering the popularity of the shoe brand, the forensic evidence was weak at best.

••••••

January 16, 1998

"I can't open it. I don't have any keys. It's on a timer!" The 62-year-old female clerk at the Canadian Imperial Bank of Commerce was terrified as the masked man pointed his sawed-off shotgun directly at her, demanding she open the safe. She was holding both hands in the air.

"Hurry up," he screamed.

The man had burst into the Grosvenor Avenue bank just after 9:30 a.m., barking out demands and pulling the gun from a white bag he was carrying. The experienced clerk, seeing they were being robbed, quickly shut the safe to prevent the man from getting any substantial sum of money.

"Shit," the man yelled, stomping the ground and turning around back out of the bank.

He was in and out within 20 seconds, fleeing empty-handed. Syrnyk was looking for a big score today and wasn't going to waste time inside the bank waiting for the timer to expire. He ran down a back lane towards his stolen red Toyota parked at the rear of a garage on Grosvenor. He jumped behind the wheel and sped off, heading north. Syrnyk had no idea he was being watched.

"I was driving to the bank and as I passed by the front on Grosvenor I saw this person come around from the side of the bank wearing a grey ski mask and a bag under his arm," the 47-year-old female motorist told the police. "At first I thought he was just cleaning the snow but then when he entered the bank I knew it was a robbery. Then when I turned the corner on to Stafford Street I saw through the windows one of the tellers put her hands into the air, so I knew it was a robbery. I parked my car behind the bank and I was going to call the police from the barbershop across the street, however, I saw the person leave the bank and return to the alley the same way that he came from, beside the bank. He came out behind the bank and got into a car that was running, in to the driver's seat." The woman said the recent murder of a young Winnipeg grocery store clerk was fresh in her mind and prevented her from getting too close. The clerk, Jeff Giles, had been shot in the face while trying to chase armed robbers who had just attacked his store. She was unable to provide a clear description of the getaway car, including a licence plate, except to say it was a red Toyota. Police broadcast a description of the getaway car over their radio, warning officers the suspect should be considered armed and dangerous. Syrnyk heard the message over the scanner and was surprised he had been seen fleeing the bank.

This kind of sloppiness was unacceptable.

● ● ● ● ● ●

Detectives in the major crime-robbery division thought they likely had a serial bandit at work, with three bank robberies in eight days. All occurred at similar times of the morning and with a comparable suspect description. This was likely the work of some junkie who was in quick need of some cash to feed his habit. Experience taught them the man would continue his pattern until he eventually got careless and was arrested.

Police hoped that would be soon, considering the man was carrying a shotgun with him, which was a recipe for disaster – especially if he was coked-up at the time.

The botched robbery hit Syrnyk hard, the confidence he had built up gone in a heartbeat.

In a moment of sheer desperation and panic he returned to his usual spot on the Assiniboine River, pulled several guns out of a bag and threw them into a watery hole he'd cut through the ice. Once again, Syrnyk was at war with himself. He decided to lay low for a while. Maybe forever.

• • • • • •

March 20, 1998

The call came into the Winnipeg police dispatch centre at exactly 9:20 a.m.. A courier driver was reporting the kind of incident that sent chills up a police officer's spine – a bank robbery was in progress. The 59-year-old man said he was about to enter the Crosstown Credit Union just minutes earlier when a masked man carrying a bag with a barrel sticking out of it had run inside. The witness had quickly retreated to his vehicle but could see what appeared to be an armed hold-up unfolding inside the bank. Calls such as this – rare as they were – had potential tragedy written all over them. Standoffs, hostage takings and gunfights were all potential results of police arriving on scene to catch a desperate armed criminal in the act. All police units in the vicinity of 1200 Henderson Highway began rushing to the scene.

The Yuletide Bandit

Syrnyk's self-imposed two-month hiatus was over. But the scene inside the bank nearly stopped him in his tracks – four customers, three of whom were carrying small children. A pang of guilt washed over Syrnyk, who never wanted to leave his mark on young victims. But the damage was already done as the gun-toting Syrnyk was now the focus of everyone inside. Especially aware was a 38-year-old secretary who had been in the same bank when it was robbed on Jan. 8. She recognized the bandit as the same man whose actions still kept her awake at night.

Syrnyk ran to the front counter, jumping over it and demanding money from the female clerk. She opened the till and he quickly grabbed a wad of bills. Syrnyk repeated this with two more tellers before jumping back over the counter and out the front door. He stumbled briefly. The last thing he saw was the terrified look of three innocent young faces.

Winnipeg police kept their flashing lights going, but turned off their sirens as they neared the bank, not wanting to signal their arrival. It was too late – the courier was now reporting the robber had just got behind the wheel of a blue Honda Accord that he had parked on nearby Hawthorne Avenue. But the alert courier had managed to move his vehicle close enough to get a peak of the licence plate – AZA 541. Police immediately set up a roadblock in the area.

Syrnyk had driven for only a few minutes when he heard his licence plate broadcast over the police airwaves. This was not good news. His second stolen car was set up quite a distance away and Syrnyk knew he couldn't wait. He was downtown, at the famous intersection of Portage and Main, and traffic was quite heavy. He continued south on Main Street figuring he'd get into the residential neighbourhood of St. Boniface, dump the car and either find another one or jump in a cab or on a bus. As he drove over the Marion Street Bridge connecting downtown with St. Boniface, Syrnyk could see a police car sitting just over the hump. It was a roadblock checkpoint and he was about to drive straight into it. Syrnyk panicked, quickly slamming on his brakes. He felt a bump as the car behind him drove right into the rear bumper. Syrnyk cranked his wheel to the left, turning his vehicle around by pulling a U-turn on the first hump of the bridge. He was now heading north on Main and it appeared the police ahead hadn't seen the bridge commotion. Another close call averted.

Police called off the roadblock about 10:15 a.m., figuring their elusive bank robber had made another clean getaway. This time the haul was just over $5,000. Major crimes detectives immediately linked the robbery to the three from January and began to think they were dealing with a polished professional rather than some down and out druggie. Unfortunately, descriptions of their suspect were all over the map painting him as tall and short, fat and thin. There was no consistency. Routine patrols of banks and surveillance of high-risk areas would have to be stepped up, especially ones that had already been hit in an attempt to thwart the man's future plans. But police knew predicting the specifics of the next target were a gamble – and this was a game they'd prefer not to be playing.

• • • • • •

March 26, 1998

The spree continued. This time, Syrnyk picked the Astra Credit Union on Ness Avenue located in the western part of Winnipeg. It was relatively close to the home he shared with his mother. Syrnyk had been careful to check for young children before he burst in through the front doors. There were only four adults inside today. He followed his normal practice of leaping over the counter to let everyone know he meant business – although the shotgun was probably a good indicator. The customers didn't know it was just loaded with rock salt. "Give me all the money," he shouted to the 19-year-old female teller, the forceful words flowing easily from his mouth now. "Is there any more?" he asked, not entirely satisfied with the small wad of bills. The teller shook her head so Syrnyk fled. Once again he had trouble with the counter, catching his foot on the edge. As he got outside the bank he noticed a young man was sitting behind the wheel of his truck parked in a nearby stall. The man seemed to be watching him. Syrnyk sensed trouble. His concerns were heightened when the man tried to start his truck, resulting in a loud grinding noise.

Syrnyk was on edge, given the recent close calls with police and wanted to let the man know he should back off and not attempt to follow him. He reached into his bag, pulling out the shotgun. Syrnyk pointed it directly at the man in the truck, holding it straight for about three seconds. He returned the gun to the bag, confident the message had been delivered that he was not to be messed with.

• • • • • •

March 27, 1998

Another call for a robbery in progress came into the police communications centre just after 11:30 a.m.. This time, the scene was the Toronto Dominion Bank on Academy Road. A man out for a walk in the area told police he saw a masked man run inside the bank, carrying a rifle or shotgun. The 911 operator called the bank and a woman answered the phone. She confirmed the robbery but said the suspect had just fled the scene.

Police arrived to find several shaken employees and customers but no sign of the serial bandit. The masked man had performed his usual feats of jumping over the counter and reaching into the till, this time taking about $2,000. Police figured they had missed him by only a minute or two.

Syrnyk dumped his getaway car within a couple blocks of the bank, learning his lesson from the recent near disaster that it wasn't wise to stay in the same car for very long. This proved to be a good move as Syrnyk heard over the police scanner that officers had recovered the first stolen vehicle within about five minutes of him dumping it behind a church near the bank. He had left it running in his haste to switch cars and police obviously hadn't fallen for the little trick he had pulled by punching the ignition, only to put the casing around the steering wheel back so it looked like he hadn't tampered with it. Fortunately for him, they had no idea what he was driving now.

• • • • • •

April 17, 1998

There was no stopping him. Syrnyk's ego was beginning to take over, a feeling that no matter what he did he was unstoppable. He had survived a few close calls and felt like he had quickly mastered the art of bank robbery. At the same time, he was finding the banks a little too routine and he wasn't enjoying scaring the women he was confronting. Or the children. He was also seeing the image of the young teller in Calgary, the tears flowing down her cheeks, and was beginning to think of other methods of getting what he wanted. Syrnyk decided today might be his swan song.

"Get the cash," he said in a calm but firm voice to the middle-aged man behind the counter. There were at least nine people inside the Assiniboine Credit Union on St. Mary's Road – a few too many for

Syrnyk's liking. He made his way to a few different tellers, grabbing cash from their tills before fleeing the bank on foot. He had made $2,335 for about 45 seconds of work.

Police canvassed the area for information, speaking with employees at a nearby gas station and hair salon. Nothing. This robbery marked eight since the beginning of the year and it seemed like there was no end in sight. A bank employee did provide a possible lead, giving officers the name of a man who had gotten into a heated argument with them weeks earlier. The man was angry the bank wouldn't cash a personal cheque for $114 because he only had a balance of $7.98 in his account. He began swearing at bank employees, then lunged at a female teller and even tried to get behind the counter. He eventually left without further incident. It was a long shot, but police were willing to take anything they could at this time. Public safety was at risk.

Michael Syrnyk fondly remembered the first time he saw a naked woman in the flesh. His father was sitting beside him. They were inside a Portage Avenue bar known to locals as The Big A, watching a parade of gorgeous young women bump and grind on stage. His dad had suggested they go for a drink after working at the butcher shop all day. It was an awakening for Syrnyk, still in his late teens and a virgin at the time, and the experience left him yearning for more.

Syrnyk's first experience with prostitutes also occurred in the company of his father, although in a much more innocent way. At the age of 19, Syrnyk wanted to look at a motorcycle at a Main Street dealership and brought his father along for guidance. As they drove through the North End, Syrnyk was in awe at the sight of numerous scantily clad women parading themselves on nearby street corners. A wide-eyed Syrnyk watched as cars slowed to a crawl and women in high heels and short, tight mini-skirts bent over to speak with the drivers. Sometimes, they would get inside the car. Syrnyk's imagination would run wild as to what the pair was about to do. He would later learn the area was known as Winnipeg's "low track", which would become somewhat of a second home to him as he eventually became a regular fixture in the city's burgeoning sex industry.

While in the company of hookers, Syrnyk often worried about disease. But his need for sex allowed him to block it out of his mind. After the deed was done, Syrnyk usually found himself scrubbing and washing compulsively, feeling emotionally fulfilled yet physically dirty all at once. He never picked up a prostitute off the street, preferring to stay indoors at massage parlours, which provided a safer, cleaner and more controlled atmosphere. For Syrnyk, sex had become a necessary outlet. There was an element of danger – not unlike the feeling just before running into a bank – which came from paying for sex. He loved the feeling of being with someone, if only for a few minutes, then being able to walk away with no strings attached. It was instant gratification. The thought of anything lasting much longer frightened Syrnyk. He had felt a slight bond with a couple of the women over the years, but nothing so strong that left him thinking the relationship was anything but business. There were times he thought about the prospects of a real relationship, but Syrnyk quickly put those delusions out of his mind, knowing his world of self-indulgent chaos was no place for a long-term romance.

The exposure to the sex trade also gave Syrnyk a peek into Winnipeg's drug culture. Offers of drugs came easier than a $20 blowjob, and yet Syrnyk had always resisted the temptation. He wanted to be in control of himself, and felt mind-altering substances would only strip him of that and leave him vulnerable.

Deep down, Syrnyk managed to maintain a high level of respect for women, despite countless faceless, sex-for-money encounters. Much of that respect came from his grandmother, a wonderful lady who had died before Syrnyk turned 10. She had been his favourite relative, a warm woman with a wicked sense of humour and so much love to go around. Syrnyk respected her more than anyone else in his life. He was devastated when she died, and always felt a small piece of him went with her. The loss only seemed greater as he aged and slowly isolated himself from his remaining family. Syrnyk often visited his grandmother's gravesite, at the Chapel Lawns Memorial Gardens cemetery on the western edge of Winnipeg. He would go alone, and spend long periods of time sitting at her tombstone, just thinking about life, enjoying the peace and quiet. He felt comfortable among the dead.

Syrnyk had been thinking a lot about his grandmother lately as he waged an internal war with himself over the wrongs he'd recently committed. Of particular concern was the amount of terrified female faces he'd encountered inside the banks. Syrnyk truly believed the majority of his robbery victims felt a similar rush as he had, and likely walked away from the experience with a newfound sense of appreciation for life. Perhaps they hugged their children a little tighter, or told a loved one how much they meant to them. But Syrnyk could see there were some who clearly didn't enjoy the experience, which took away much of his own satisfaction. The young girl in Calgary who wouldn't stop crying. The woman in Winnipeg with the little children. What had they thought when they went home that night? Were they able to sleep? Would they ever recover? Syrnyk often lay awake at night, his overactive mind unable to stop focusing on the crying faces. He found himself slipping further into depression.

Although the temporary high that came with the bank robberies gave him a brief reprieve, Syrnyk's conscience was getting to him. Syrnyk had never laid his hands on a woman in a violent way, and yet his actions inside the banks certainly implied violence. He didn't believe in victimizing people who he viewed as weaker than him, and women and children fell into that category. It was time to start moving away from banks, and re-focus his efforts on going after men. The challenge would be greater. But at least it would be fair.

• • • • • •

Thoughts of suicide were becoming increasingly prevalent. Syrnyk was routinely having visions of walking into a deeply wooded area, finding a comfortable spot among the trees, and ending his life with a bullet to the brain. It seemed so peaceful, so serene. But these were crazy thoughts, which Syrnyk, after a while, put out of his head.

But another demon was suddenly making things more difficult – alcohol. At first, it was just a couple drinks every few days. But Syrnyk quickly found that wasn't enough to mask his suffering, drown it really, and began drinking to the point of excess on most days. The short term numbing would be erased by pangs of guilt, paranoid thoughts and delusions, and increasing worry and depression. So he'd drink some more, and the cycle would continue. Brent Syrnyk knew there was something very wrong with his brother, and yet Syrnyk was offering little insight into his obviously troubled world. The two brothers were now living together in a small apartment, although Syrnyk would often go stay with their mother for several days at a time, or not come home at all on other occasions.

Brent had seen a dramatic change in Syrnyk in recent months, one that he struggled to understand. Syrnyk had always loved his privacy, dating back to their childhood years spent at the family cottage on Rice Lake near Bissett, Manitoba. The Syrnyk boys would often ride their bicycles together, but Syrnyk always wanted to press on. An exhausted Brent would head inside while Syrnyk stayed outside for another few hours, alone, just exploring the wilderness. By the end of a day, Syrnyk had often pedaled 20 miles or more. The boys loved all aspects of nature, from canoeing to hiking and exploring. Syrnyk was especially fond of searching out new paths and adventures in the bush, and would go off by himself for the bulk of the day. He'd return, scrapes and bug bites all over his body, but say little about where he'd been or what he'd done. That was just the way he was.

In their early teens, Syrnyk had bought some books on gardening and how to build a log cabin. It was his dream to live the life of a bushman, surviving off the land and becoming one with nature. He would joke with Brent, saying he wanted to live like a Buddhist. "All I need is a wooden bowl and a spoon," he would say. Syrnyk was very minimalist, not wanting much more than the clothes on his back. "What is real is what's inside of you," he often told Brent. That's the way Syrnyk was, a sense of humour that not only made you laugh, but also think. He was loyal to a fault, and had filled his head with a wealth of knowledge from the books he poured himself into, and his life experiences. Syrnyk always had a soft spot for animals, and was extremely vocal in his contempt for people who abused them. Based largely on his own experience at home, Syrnyk also had strong views against child and spousal abuse, and often told Brent what he saw in life "sickened" him. Brent figured this contributed largely to his withdrawal from crowds and the anti-social behaviours Syrnyk had developed. It seemed like he no longer wanted to be around people.

Fearing his brother was coming apart, Brent tried to take Syrnyk to see a doctor. It was a difficult subject to broach, with the Syrnyk boys being raised in a home by a father who didn't exactly preach the virtues of wearing your emotions on your sleeve. If you had a problem, you dealt with it. Better if it was on your own time, in your own way. Syrnyk originally resisted Brent's pleadings, but his respect for his brother ultimately gave way and the boys walked into the Misericordia Hospital together one evening. With no mental health specialist on sight, the on-call doctor simply gave Syrnyk a free sample of the anti-depressant drug Paxil, booked him an appointment with a social worker and sent him on his way. Syrnyk threw the drugs away, refusing to take them. "I don't want to walk around like a zombie," he told Brent. The experience only seemed to further alienate Syrnyk, and Brent worried what was becoming of his brother.

●●●●●●

They were known as the Stopwatch Gang – a rogue band of sophisticated bank robbers who prided themselves on getting in and out in two minutes or less. Canadian Stephen Reid was the leader of a three-man crew that stole $15 million from more than 150 banks across North America in the 1960s and 1970s. With a timepiece hanging from his neck, Reid tried to keep his victims relaxed by calmly assuring them "This won't take long, folks." The gang used guns, but weren't strong proponents of violence. Their robberies were meticulously planned and executed, designed to capture as much money as possible in the least amount of time with no gunplay or injuries. Reid, along with Paddy Mitchell and Lionel Wright, once made off with $750,000 in gold during a hold-up job in Ottawa. The Stopwatch Gang committed the largest robbery in California history by walking off with $283,000 from a San Diego bank in 1980. The heist landed them on the FBI's Most Wanted List. Between "gigs", the Stopwatch Gang lived in a luxurious glass and cedar home in the Arizona mountains. They told neighbours they were concert promoters. Reid befriended some of the locals, even playing regular bridge games with the local sheriff. The gang's bizarre double-life came to an end in 1980, shortly after the San Diego robbery, when police linked them to the dozens of unsolved cases. Reid was sentenced to 14 years in prison, but put the time to good use. He wrote a novel, *Jackrabbit Parole*, based on his criminal conquests while doing time at Millhaven penitentiary.

Michael Syrnyk knew the story of Stephen Reid and the Stopwatch Gang very well. They were his heroes. Syrnyk had spent countless hours reading up to the exploits of the Stopwatch Gang, mostly through old clippings and microfiche at the Winnipeg Public Library. *Those guys were tight*, he often thought to himself. *There was a real sense of honour among those guys.* Like an actor would study old clips of Hollywood stars from the past, Syrnyk knew there were great lessons to be learned from successful crimes of the past.

With several bank robberies under his belt, Syrnyk became a regular fixture at the library, digging up as many articles as he could find on major heists

The Yuletide Bandit

from around the world. He began spending several hours each day staring at a computer screen or dropping coins into the photocopy machine so he could bring his research home with him. The articles, combined with his Palladin Press "how-to" books, made for quite a collection. But Syrnyk knew experience was his best teacher. And as much as stories of successful bank robberies intrigued him, Syrnyk was becoming increasingly interested in another type of crime. The art of the armoured car hold-up.

CHAPTER 6

July 1998

Dressed completely in black, Michael Syrnyk crept carefully around the side of the garage, making sure nobody was watching. Most lights inside the house were off, which certainly reduced the risk. It was 11 p.m., and traffic on the street was light. Once he had climbed to the roof Syrnyk slithered over towards the front edge, where he could have a good look at the bank across the street. It was a CIBC, located at the corner of Grosvenor Avenue and Stafford Street. Syrnyk had picked this location to be the scene of his first armoured car heist mainly because of his fondness for a large shrub just to the left of the front entrance, which provided the perfect cover. Because the element of surprise was his key to success, Syrnyk needed to keep out of sight as long as possible. He took a firm position on the roof, making sure to keep himself as close to the shingles as possible. His cold eyes began darting from side to side, surveying the area. He felt powerful, like a wild animal stalking its unsuspecting prey. Just after 11, Syrnyk spotted his targets pulling up in their large, fortified Loomis truck. One guard got out, followed by another. A third appeared to stay inside the vehicle. He couldn't see their faces. It would be easier that way. *These are my targets, these are not people anymore. I need their money*, Syrnyk said to himself, a cryptic mantra he would repeat nearly every night for the next three weeks as he painstakingly followed the same routine. Each and every night, Syrnyk immediately fixed his sights on the bag one guard was carrying. Another guard would always accompany the bag holder, keeping a lookout. The mantra continued. *These are obstacles in my way. My life means more than theirs. I need that bag.*

It was early August now, and Syrnyk had finally had enough. He had watched the guards conduct the same routine for so many nights that there was nothing left to learn. He knew their routes like clockwork. He had psyched himself up as much as he could. What was he waiting for? *Stop being a bitch and get on with it*, Syrnyk shouted at himself.

• • • • • •

Becoming an armed guard in Canada requires little more than a birth certificate and a two-day firearms safety course. Top pay is in the range of $15 an hour, and the risk is that someone will try to shoot you. The Canadian Firearms Centre, which licences armoured guards to carry weapons, has a simple process to get your gun – all armoured guards must have a firearms possession and acquisitions certificate. Companies such as Loomis, Brink's and Securicor must provide documentation to the firearms centre to prove a guard has been provided with a minimum two-day training course in firearms safety before the licence will be granted. The security companies conduct the courses in-house. The only other requirements are that the guard be over 18 years of age and without a criminal record. Most companies offer a yearly refresher course, but a large job turnover because of the low wages and high risk renders the process moot in many cases. The issue has long been a touchy one in Canada, with union leaders who represent armoured car guards calling on the government to increase the amount of training armed guards receive. But with only a handful of incidents each year across the country, the issue isn't seen as a top priority for federal lawmakers.

August 9, 1998

The Loomis truck approached the CIBC bank right at 11 p.m. – the normal arrival time for what was specifically referred to by the armoured car company as "run number five". Allan Wiebe was behind the wheel, while Mike Bosek and Shauna Martens were the passenger seats. The trio were working the overnight shift, from 9:30 p.m. to 5:30 a.m.. They had already done a pickup at the Toronto Dominion bank on Academy Road with no problems. Their route would take them to some of the wealthier areas of the city tonight. Wiebe had just started working for

Loomis 10 days earlier, and had been filling in with Martens and Bosek because the regular driver was on holidays. This was to be their last night working together. Martens' first shift had only been a month ago. Bosek was the veteran, having been employed for all of two years. Wiebe pulled the truck on to Stafford, just south of Grosvenor. He would wait inside while Bosek and Martens went inside the bank. Their task was simply to pick up the night deposits.

Martens had the keys and opened the glass double door to the bank, being careful to lock it as she and Bosek went inside. Bosek was carrying a green canvas bag, while Martens had a red and green one. The pair spent the next 15 minutes inside, collecting deposits and placing them inside the bags. On this night, approximately $6,400 was there waiting. After a final check, they prepared to leave. Bosek stood guard in the vestibule housing the automated teller machines as Martens waited for the exterior doors to self-close behind her. Bosek took a quick peek around the area and saw nothing unusual. Martens held open the door as Bosek walked out, now carrying both bags in his left hand. Being a right-handed shot, Bosek always kept his right hand clear in case he needed to pull his gun. As it had been seven years since an armoured car was held-up in Winnipeg, he knew that was an unlikely occurrence.

Syrnyk was covered in his own sweat, crouched underneath a large black bed sheet. He was lying facedown in the bushes just beside the bank, the ones that had caught his eyes when he was trying to select a location for the biggest heist of his short career. Syrnyk's eyes peered out from behind a black balaclava. The air was sweetly warm and humid. His baggy black pants and black sweater were adding to his discomfort. He had watched moments earlier as the Loomis guards pulled up to the bank, one waiting inside the truck while the other two walked inside the bank with the empty bags. They were right on time.

Syrnyk thought back to the day he first envisioned doing an armoured car robbery. It seemed like such a long time ago, that lunch hour at the butcher shop with his father when he'd glanced at the newspaper on the table and read the small item about a robbery in Ontario. *Those guys were so cool, they just walked up with their guns and started to smash the crap outta the guards, and walked off with a quarter mill,* Syrnyk had thought to himself. As impressed as he was, Syrnyk never thought he had it in him to pull off a similar feat. Yet here he was, lying beneath a sheet, waiting to pounce. He wondered what the newspapers would say about him tomorrow.

Syrnyk loaded the 12-gauge slugs into his sawed-off pump action shotgun, his steady hands in no way indicative of the inner turmoil he was struggling with. It was the first time he was using real ammunition. He was armed and ready, yet battling some last-second hesitation. Syrnyk had spent much of his life alone and in the dark, just as he was right now, yet he never remembered feeling quite as lonely or scared. Suicidal or homicidal? Syrnyk felt like he wanted someone to die tonight.

As he watched the two guards prepare to leave the bank with the bags, Syrnyk began to lose control, his hands starting to shake and the beads of sweat collecting beneath his mask. In a moment of sheer desperation, he dropped to his knees, looked up to the sky and began shouting at God in his own mind. "Why am I doing this, why am I here, why am I so fucked up?" he wailed. Predictably, there was no answer. Syrnyk didn't relent. His inner voice became angrier, demanding that God answer him. With one hand on his shotgun, Syrnyk threatened to kill everyone – himself, the guards, even God. His pulse was racing, his breathing more laboured and intense. He had mere seconds to decide what to do; yet God was nowhere to be found. As usual, Syrnyk felt all alone.

With the bank now locked, Bosek turned right and began walking north towards Stafford, where Wiebe was waiting with the truck. Martens took a position directly behind Bosek, scanning the scene as her partner walked briskly. This was always a nervous walk, as the thick bushes on the left side of the entrance prompted a fear of the unknown. Other Loomis guards had warned Bosek and Martens to be extra careful because of the cover the eight-foot tall bushes provide. Bosek had some first-hand experience, having been startled in the past by stray dogs that came running out, causing a frightening false alarm he'd rather not experience again. As they walked past the bushes, Bosek and Martens heard rustling behind them. Both turned to see a dark figure crouched down near the edge, quickly rising and now charging towards them. Syrnyk knew he had to go on the offensive. He had the element of surprise on his side, yet the guards' reaction was the wildcard. Would they simply put their hands in the air and drop the bag? Or would raw human emotion and adrenaline kick in? Syrnyk knew his gun was the best way to make a statement, and he was going to be very clear about his intentions. There would be no misunderstandings.

The first thing Bosek noticed, in fact the only thing he could see, were two small eyeholes in the balaclava and the silver end of a gun barrel pointed directly at him. It was only eight feet away. Bosek instinctively drew his .38 calibre handgun from the right holster. "Look out," screamed Martens. She still had the bank keys in her hand and ran back to the front door, hoping to take cover inside. The key briefly stuck in the lock, and Martens fumbled with it for a few seconds before opening the door.

Syrnyk jumped up from the warm ground and immediately targeted the bigger guard who was holding the two money bags. He wasted no time in squeezing the trigger. Suddenly, everything seemed to go into slow motion. As he fired, the shotgun suddenly jerked to the side. *What the hell?* Syrnyk didn't think he'd moved his hand, at least not consciously. The pellets narrowly missed hitting the guard, soaring over his shoulder, past the parked Loomis van and into a brick wall across the street more than 100 feet away

Martens was safely inside the main branch area, having secured all the doors behind her. She ran to the first telephone she could see and dialled 911, frantically describing the chaotic scene outside. Martens was desperately worried about the safety of her partner. The popping sound and white flash that exploded from the end of the masked man's gun stunned Bosek. His gun was shoulder height, and Bosek fired back, aiming towards the centre of mass of the masked gunman. He had no idea where his bullet went. Bosek ran towards the truck, looking back over his shoulder to see what the gunman was doing. Bosek stumbled over some rocks, dropping both canvas bags and falling to the ground, hitting his right knee hard. He jumped up, oblivious to the pain of a scraped left elbow and banged up knee, and ran hard towards the rear of the bank. He turned the corner and slipped and fell once again.

Syrnyk, unhurt, trained his gun at the guard, but it jammed as he tried to fire once more in his direction. He pulled out his backup gun, a .45-calibre Beretta that had concealed in his pants. Syrnyk briefly lost sight of the guard, but was more interested now in the two bags lying on the ground. He grabbed them both, then continued to search for the guard who'd just tried to shoot him. Syrnyk had thrown out all rational thought at this point. Murder was on his mind.

The Yuletide Bandit

A frantic Bosek got up off the ground once again and ran to the far corner of the bank, a crucial mistake as the area was a fenced-in dead end. He tried to climb up, but couldn't make it. Bosek had no idea where the gunman was, but knew he had to stay out of sight. Bosek crouched down in the lane, taking some comfort in the fact there was no light shining on this place of refuge. His only hope was to try and blend in with the night. His heart skipped a beat when he saw the gunman come running around the corner, stopping briefly to look his way. The man was still holding a gun, with both hands, waist high, pointed in the direction of Bosek. The frightened guard kept his eyes trained on the shiny weapon as it darted back and forth several times, as if scanning the area.

Syrnyk's search for the guard was interrupted by a call over his police scanner. Police were on their way. With one guard inside the bank and the other one apparently hiding, Syrnyk didn't have any more time to waste. He was on an emotional high, the robbery and shootout apparently wiping out the feelings of despair from only moments earlier. With the money bags in tow, he sprinted down a lane, towards his waiting vehicle.

Bosek had just been granted a stay of execution.

CHAPTER **7**

The cemetery was quiet as usual. Michael Syrnyk sat by his grandmother's gravesite, the two bags of money sitting beside him. Syrnyk took a sip of Gibson's whisky, a drink he'd grown to like in recent months. It went down extra smooth tonight. Like a true professional, he'd left his getaway car in a ball of flames, ensuring he didn't leave any evidence behind. The weeks of planning had paid off, although Syrnyk wished the haul could have been bigger. He thought again of the Loblaws heist he'd read about years earlier while cutting meat with his dad, realizing he'd come nowhere near matching their $250,000 haul. In fact, he was $244,000 short.

Syrnyk thought of the Stopwatch Gang, and the millions they had raked in over the years. The initial buzz was beginning to wear off, and Syrnyk was quickly sinking back into a depression. What exactly had he accomplished? He replayed every millisecond of the robbery back in his mind, constantly going back to the moment in time where he'd fired his gun. Syrnyk was at a loss to explain what had happened, his hand suddenly jerking to the side as he fired. He knew one thing – the shot wasn't meant to miss. Or was it? Was it just nerves? A last second change of heart? Or had God heard his cries for help and intervened?

• • • • • •

His nerves still frazzled, Mike Bosek told police how professional the gunman seemed – very deliberate in his actions as if a veteran of this type of crime. Nearly a dozen officers had rushed to the scene, quickly surrounding the bank with yellow tape. Investigators took the shaken Loomis guards on a walk around the crime scene, re-enacting what had just occurred. It was a difficult experience for all involved. A Loomis supervisor arrived at the bank, speaking with all three of his employees. It was an employer's worst nightmare come true. The supervisor told his staff to take a few days off and to register for company stress counselling the following morning. They would definitely need it.

Police searched the area for clues, the most obvious being in the bushy area where they found several flowers and plants trampled by the suspect. They looked for signs of blood, but didn't find any. The bandit had likely got away without being hit. Police found a black bed sheet draped over a fence on the west side of the bank and seized it for further examination. Several shotgun waddings and slugs were also scattered nearby. Officers canvassed several homes in the area, with residents reporting the sound of gunshots. Some thought there had been a car accident. "I was upstairs in my home, sewing. I heard a God-awful crash. It sounded like some sort of impact," a middle-aged woman told police. She had looked out her window, and saw what was believed to be the suspect vehicle fleeing from the scene. Her description was very limited and not of any assistance. Police figured their culprit knew what he was doing.

• • • • • •

Despite its dramatics, the robbery barely registered on the radar of Winnipeg's media. A few television stations mentioned it on their Monday newscasts. In a medium that thrives on pictures, the late-night robbery hadn't exactly been media-friendly. Not to mention the bank surveillance cameras only caught the sight of Martens running inside the bank, but none of the real action. The city's two daily newspapers provided few details to their readers in their Tuesday morning editions. The *Winnipeg Free Press* story was on page 6. It was the lead item in a series of police briefs that were too short to even include the writer's name on top. *"Two bandits remain at large after a hold-up of Loomis armed guards in which two shots were fired. Two Loomis guards were leaving the CIBC branch at Grosvenor Avenue and Stafford Street at 11:20 p.m. Sunday when a masked man with a sawed-off shotgun confronted them and demanded the money bags. The robber fired a shot at the guards, who fired one in return. "It's amazing that neither one was struck at such close range," said Winnipeg Police Service spokesman Sgt. Carl Shier. The robber got away with one bag. Police refused to say how much money was in the bag. It's been seven years since the last time armed guards were robbed in Winnipeg. The man ran to a waiting car, possibly a Dodge Neon. Police believe a second suspect was driving the getaway car. Shier would not say if the robber is suspected of having inside information on the guards' schedule, but did say such a robbery is likely well planned. He suggested the robber may have planned to fire his gun to scare the guards and was surprised when fire was returned. Loomis Armoured Car Service spokesman Ron Halford did not return repeated calls. The suspect is described as a stocky male, 5'9 tall and weighing 210 pounds. He wore black clothing, including a balaclava.*

Syrnyk had once again created a jackpot for himself. There had been too many days of self-doubt and pity, too many trips to the river to dump his guns in a misguided attempt to clear his conscience. Now ready to strike again, Syrnyk was nearly weaponless. As the days grew shorter and summer turned to fall in Winnipeg, Syrnyk began focusing his mind away from feelings of guilt and shame. He wanted another armoured car. Only this time, Syrnyk wasn't going to settle for a measly few thousand dollars. With the right amount of planning, and some better timing, Syrnyk figured snagging the "big one" wouldn't be a problem. Like the Stopwatch Gang, Syrnyk was ready to enter the major leagues.

●●●●●●

The Yuletide Bandit

October 15, 1998

The Farmer's Supply store was moderately busy for a Thursday evening, with nearly two dozen customers browsing the aisles or waiting in the checkout line. It was dark outside, just after 7:30 p.m., the daytime hours disappearing as fast as the leaves on the trees. Leonard Jackson and his two children, aged 16 and 12, had entered the Nairn Avenue store moments earlier. They were standing in the middle of an aisle, browsing for some hunting supplies, when the routine shopping trip took a shocking turn. Jackson and his kids heard a commotion near the front of the store. The family looked up to see a masked man confronting one of the young store clerks. He was holding a shotgun in his hand. "Don't test me, don't anybody test me!" the man shouted. Several customers cowered in the aisles, panic written across their faces. Jackson, 43, and his kids froze as the man began heading their way. "Don't anybody try and follow me," the gunman told everyone within earshot, waving his weapon around in the air. Nobody did. Several people close to the man took a few cautious steps backwards. The gunman ran behind a counter and reached for two shotguns on a shelf, grabbing both of them with one hand. His other hand kept a tight grip on the gun he'd brought into the store. Jackson noticed the man had a black hooded sweatshirt pulled up over his head, which was already covered by a balaclava. He thought the man's eyes looked light coloured, maybe blue. Definitely very cold and steely. The man worked quick, heading straight for the exit doors now carrying three guns. He issued a final warning to his victims to not follow him. He disappeared into the night, and everyone remained still.

Syrnyk was thrilled with the catch. And the execution had been flawless. *In and out, nobody got hurt – just like it should be*, he thought. Syrnyk had gone into the gun store with his weapon loaded with rock salt. Fortunately, everyone listened to him and things had gone perfectly. He was proud of himself for taking a direct approach – not shying away from confrontation, but not revelling in it either. He was intimidating, but efficient. Syrnyk picked the Farmer's Supply store because he liked the cover provided by the back of the building, which was dark and empty. He had parked his stolen car there to ensure a quick getaway. Both shotguns he grabbed were 12-gauge Remingtons. Syrnyk was especially fond of one that was camouflaged. The other was nickel-plated. In just a short time, Syrnyk was becoming a connoisseur of guns. From visiting the gun shops of Calgary to reading numerous books and articles, he was a quick study. Syrnyk knew these shotguns were too good to throw into the river and vowed to hold on to them. He planned to be very busy, and their services would definitely be required.

Syrnyk, his mind still very much focused on the Stopwatch Gang, was also beginning to have thoughts of bringing someone else into his troubled world. As a private person all his life, Syrnyk didn't have any trouble acting alone. But he found himself wondering what it would be like to have a partner, someone with whom he could share in the planning, someone he could both teach and learn from. The thought of confiding in someone was frightening, yet exhilarating. If he ever did find a confidante, Syrnyk vowed it would be a seasoned professional, someone who knew what they were doing and wouldn't drag him down. And yet, Syrnyk realized he had already gone where few criminals in Winnipeg had before. Nobody was doing armoured cars, which meant anyone he brought into the mix would be a student to his teachings. Syrnyk planned to give the idea more thought, but put it out of his head for now. He had other things to think about. Christmas was coming, and that meant big money.

• • • • • •

December 21, 1998

Syrnyk pulled into the parking lot of the Grant Park Shopping Centre just after noon, finding a parking space in front of the Wal-Mart store but still a good distance away from the front doors. He'd stolen his white, four-door 1989 Honda Accord three days earlier. Syrnyk sat inside the vehicle, alone, watching people of all shapes and sizes coming and going from the busy mall. The Christmas rush was in full swing. But Syrnyk didn't just see people on this day. He saw cash, and lots of it. For the past couple weeks he had meticulously planned what was going to be his most lucrative crime to date. Cash registers work overtime in the weeks before Christmas, and most stores were dealing with cash flows that far surpass the other 11 months of the year. Syrnyk had followed the Loomis armoured car on its daily run several times, knowing precisely when they'd arrive, where they were coming from, how long they'd take inside the mall and where they were headed next. He'd set up two other stolen cars, mapping out his escape route to perfection. One was parked in an alcove, just across the parking lot. That would be his getaway car. The other was halfway across the city, on Church Avenue, just waiting for his arrival.

As the clock ticked down towards 1 p.m., Syrnyk tensed up. One of the Remington shotguns was slung across his chest, underneath his bulky red and black parka. Syrnyk checked to make sure it was secured. He had a handgun in his possession as well. That was going to be his weapon of choice. The shotgun was simply insurance. Syrnyk could see the Loomis truck driving into the lot. He reached to the side and grabbed his black balaclava with his gloved hands, slipping it over his head.

Ronald Buck began working with Loomis only six months earlier, as a means to earn some extra cash and gain some valuable experience. He had spent the past six years working as an auxiliary policeman in a small community just outside of Winnipeg and had dreams of one day becoming a full-fledged cop in a big city.

The Yuletide Bandit

Single and living with his brother, Buck was happy with the part-time armoured car work, despite the obvious safety concerns. He knew about the August robbery from his co-workers, a reminder that you always had to be on guard. He was the driver – remaining behind while his partner went inside – but Buck took some comfort in the handgun he was carrying. Buck's partner today was Gerard Lesage, a veteran employee who had changed careers following 10 years installing windows. He was married with a young child and a fun guy to be around. They were expecting a busy shift.

Buck pulled the Loomis van in front of Wal-Mart, their twelfth stop of a crazy day which had only begun three hours earlier. It was 1:10 p.m. Lesage got out, took a look around and proceeded to the back. He pulled out a large bag of coins, placing it on a trolley because it was too heavy to carry. He walked into the store, leaving Buck behind in the truck. Lesage went directly to the upstairs main office, dropping off the cash delivery. In exchange, he was given a large cash deposit which he placed inside a canvas bag. Lesage returned to the main floor area, now wheeling the empty trolley and carrying the bag. He left through the main doors, stopping briefly for oncoming traffic and continued on to the Loomis van. It was 1:15 p.m.. Lesage stood the trolley up to the back door of the vehicle, reaching into his pocket for the keys to open it. The bag was still in one hand when the masked man suddenly jumped out from the side of the van.

"Drop the bag!" Syrnyk ordered the middle-aged guard, pointing the handgun directly at the guard's lower body. The man didn't move. "Drop the fucking bag," Syrnyk repeated, his voice louder and more serious this time. Syrnyk could see several people standing around near the front of the store and knew that it wouldn't be long until somebody called police. He had to move fast. The guard finally listened, dropping the sack to the ground. Syrnyk scooped it up, keeping his eyes and gun trained on the guard. He wasn't finished. "Give me your gun," he said. Syrnyk still felt like he needed more guns. The guard now had his hands in the air. But he didn't budge. Syrnyk was getting angry. He moved in, standing directly on the right side of the man, pressing the gun against his body. Syrnyk reached into the guard's holster and pulled. The gun didn't move. He tried again, with the same result. That was enough. Rather than stay and fight, Syrnyk gave up and began running towards the main entrance of the mall. He planned to cut through and exit out the back so he could get to his waiting vehicle. As he got to the front doors, Syrnyk turned back to look at the Loomis guard, who was still standing beside the truck. Syrnyk pointed his gun one more time at the man, a reminder he meant business, then turned and ran into Wal-Mart.

"Ronald. Holy fuck!" Lesage shouted, pounding on the back of the Loomis van. Buck looked out and saw a commotion near the front of the mall as a masked man ran through the front doors. He remained inside the vehicle, as per company policy. Lesage ran to the driver's side window, quickly telling his partner he was okay. He appeared calm. As Buck began calling in the robbery, Lesage ran towards the mall. His gun was drawn.

Calls were pouring into the Winnipeg Police Service about a brazen, daytime robbery that had just gone down in a parking lot filled with Christmas shoppers. One caller said he'd just watched a masked man run out of a Honda Accord, towards the mall, waving a gun. He said the vehicle was still in the parking lot, still running. Every available police unit in the city began speeding towards the mall.

Winnipeg paramedic Stan Stone had just been heading into Wal-Mart when the masked bandit ran by, brushing his shoulder and knocking him to the side. As one of the city's paramedic supervisors, Stone had witnessed a lot of crazy things in his career – violent, aggressive patients, deadly car accidents and too many gruesome injuries to count. Stone had built up somewhat of an immunity to chaos, because he lived it almost every day. Although he was shocked at the sight of a gunman running by him, Stone had no hesitation in making his next move. He began following the man. The guard who'd just been robbed quickly joined Stone, and together they ran through Wal-Mart.

"Where did he go? Did you see him?" Lesage asked everyone in their path. Several confused customers pointed out the man's route of travel. A third man joined in the chase, having jumped out of the way as the suspect ran down an aisle in the store. He initially thought he was running after a teen shoplifter. Then he heard somebody say the man had a gun. Stone pulled out his cellular phone and was trying to get through to 911, but the line was busy. Stone and Lesage were in the shoe section of Wal-Mart when several people told them the man had just fled through a door. The pair raced outside, where several other people were standing. They said the man had continued down the back lane, heading south, then west through a yard. He was out of sight. Stone gave up the chase, giving Lesage his business card and heading home. Amid all the confusion, he had forgotten why he'd come to the store in the first place and left empty-handed. Lesage briefly continued his foot pursuit, getting as far as the yard but turning around when he couldn't see anything. He walked back to the mall to wait for police.

Police brought in extra units in from other districts and called in officers who were off-duty. They needed all the help they could get. Major crimes detectives quickly arrived on scene, suspecting the same culprit from August had struck again. Only this time, the payoff had been much bigger. The two Loomis victims estimated there was nearly $60,000 cash inside the bag.

Police recovered the stolen vehicle in the parking lot, hauling it to the Public Safety Building for a thorough forensic examination. Most witnesses described the suspect as being in the range of 5'8 to 5'11, of average build. An elderly couple thought it could be a female, claiming the culprit "walked like a woman." Police disregarded that information, convinced the bandit was a man. Police cordoned off the scene where the suspect was last seen, awaiting the arrival of the canine unit to attempt a track.

The dog picked up an initial scent in the yard, running quickly with his nose to the ground. Several officers followed, their guns drawn. The track abruptly ended at the street, where police believed the man might have fled into a car. The ground search was called off. It picked up again just before 3 p.m. when a caller told police they'd seen a person running across some nearby train tracks, just behind a gas station. Police flooded the area, but quickly established the "suspect" was just a woman out for a jog with her dog. Back at the scene, Lesage was asked by police to re-enact the robbery in hopes it would provide additional clues. He began the painful process of re-living the most frightening experience of his life.

• • • • • •

With a whisky in his belly and a smile on his face, Syrnyk gleefully went through the Loomis bag like a kid at Christmas. This was more like it. Not only had he hit the proverbial jackpot, but the incident had gone down as planned with no violence required.

Unlike the guard in August, this one kept his gun in his holster and smartly complied with Syrnyk's orders. Syrnyk poured another drink and toasted the birth of the Yuletide Bandit.

CHAPTER 8

Winnipeg police were dealing with a public relations nightmare – a trigger-happy bandit who had shifted away from working under the cover of darkness and appeared to relish the grand stage that a daytime heist presented. And just days before Christmas, no less, in front of dozens of horrified witnesses who might never recover from the holiday trauma. Police refused to overlook any theory on the robber's identity, no matter how far-fetched. Officers from around the city, whatever their rank or experience, were encouraged to keep their eyes open and their ideas flowing as to who might be responsible. These were desperate times, with car companies, store merchants and regular citizens on edge and demanding answers. If the bandit had any fears, he certainly wasn't showing them. With the man clearly not concerned about large crowds or using his weapon, police knew there was a tragedy waiting to happen if an arrest didn't come soon.

Christmas 1998 came to pass with no further incidents, hardly a surprise given the large financial gain the gunman had received. It was becoming evident to police their culprit was choosing his targets carefully, and likely putting some thought and planning into his crimes. A pattern was also developing, with major crimes detectives becoming increasingly certain the same bandit might also be responsible for several of the unsolved bank robberies from recent years. Although the suspect descriptions varied slightly from crime to crime, there were similarities that couldn't be overlooked and suggested an escalating pattern of violence.

Fortunately, Winnipeg didn't have an obscene amount of unsolved robberies – or an endless pool of potential suspects – which made narrowing down comparisons much easier. However, police were striking out in the forensic evidence department, as a thorough analysis of the bandit's seized stolen car revealed nothing in the way of fingerprints, hair or fibres. If all these crimes were linked, the bandit had clearly progressed from simple note jobs to gunpoint confrontations to night-time surprise attacks to brazen daytime jobs. What would be his next step? It was unlikely their suspect was some crackhead looking for quick cash to feed his addiction. Still, police didn't want to rule anything out. With that in mind, officers set their sights on a well-known local hoodlum who piqued their interests for a number of reasons. First, the man had a similar physical appearance to the culprit described by most of the witnesses at the Grant Park Wal-Mart. Second, the man lived relatively close to the store location, which could explain the quick getaway. And while he had no prior history of being an armoured car thief, police thought he might have decided to elevate his criminal behaviour to a new level. It was worth taking a look at.

So, in the days following the Christmas robbery, police set up surveillance on the man's home. They watched. And they watched. And they watched. While the man was often in their sights, he certainly wasn't acting like someone who had just won the lottery or was on the run from police. Senior police investigators eventually pulled the plug on the undercover operation. Precious man-hours were being eaten away by the fruitless surveillance, and further review and reflection diminished their theory the man might be involved.

Police began exploring the remote possibility the Christmas heist could be an inside job, perhaps connected to some disgruntled Wal-Mart employee looking to make a healthy year-end bonus with the help of some shady friend. As a precaution, police obtained a list of all employees working at the store at the time. It was a long shot, but police felt it was worth running some names on the computer system just to see if anything of interest popped up. But after many hours spent pouring through names and conducting background checks, it became apparent police were heading down another dead-end street.

• • • • • •

January 10, 1999

It was the most interesting tip Winnipeg police had received to date. Two Loomis guards not connected with either of the first two robberies walked into the Public Safety Building just after 8:30 p.m. to discuss the ongoing investigation. The pair believed they were going to be the next victims.

Both guards explained how they thought they were being followed while driving one of their regular night time bank routes, near St. Mary's Road and Poplarwood Avenue in the south end of the city. For several days running, they had noticed the same two cars were always in the area of the bank, parked and running, at the same time. Could the bandit be planning his next attack?

Police acted quickly, scrambling a team of undercover officers together to set up surveillance of the Loomis guards doing their nightly run. The guards had partial descriptions of both cars – a black Jeep Cherokee and a blue Ford Explorer. The operation began immediately, as the Loomis guards left the downtown police station and headed back out to continue their shift. Several unmarked cruiser cars followed closely behind. It was midnight – just as the guards had said – when the two cars appeared in the distance. Police prepared to move in.

Officers got close enough to obtain the licence plates and quickly ran them through their computer system. The results were most puzzling. Their "targets" were a couple of middle-aged, law-abiding suburbanites. One man and one woman. Not exactly the suspect description they had in mind. It got worse. With their guns at the ready, police approached the vehicles with caution. As it turned out, there certainly was some illicit activity going on. Both individuals were married – but not to each other.

In their haste to catch a serial criminal police had stumbled across an extra-marital affair in progress that certainly wasn't grounds to lock anybody up. Police let the lovebirds carry on, affairs of the heart not requiring any further investigation. The Loomis guards thanked police for their efforts and continued on their way, feeling slightly embarrassed but also more secure in knowing their route was apparently safe.

••••••

Vancouver, British Columbia

The rain, it seemed, would never end. Nor would Michael Syrnyk's personal agony. He'd come to the west coast of Canada early in the New Year, buying a one-way bus ticket on a whim and only telling his family he was going away for a while. His parents, and especially Brent, were obviously concerned, but Syrnyk wasn't in the mood for explanations or discussions. As usual, the good vibes of the successful armoured car heist had worn off, and Syrnyk was feeling an even deeper low than ever before. Syrnyk checked into a seedy Vancouver motel, hardly the accommodations befitting a man who'd just come into $60,000 cash. He'd made a good year's salary in the space of five minutes, but Syrnyk wasn't about to start living large. It wasn't in his nature.

Before heading west, Syrnyk had stepped up his visits to Winnipeg massage parlours, giving the friendly girls a little extra for their services. It was the least he could for all they'd done for him over the years. But now he was alone, spending the majority of the gloomy, soggy days sitting inside his rundown room, stamping out the occasional cockroach. However, Syrnyk had discovered a new friend – marijuana.

He'd fought the urge in the past, but finally gave in to temptation, hoping to help curb his emotional roller coaster. For the most part, pot was doing a good job in helping to mellow him out and turn terrible days into simply bad ones. It also took away his regular thirst for sex, a sort of "vice for a vice" exchange. Syrnyk would occasionally get angry with himself for putting the drug into his system, but would usually quell those feelings by smoking a joint or two. *Who really gives a fuck?* he often thought while taking a drag.

Syrnyk occasionally left his motel room, taking long walks through Vancouver. He was getting to know the city, but not its people. Syrnyk avoided going into bars and massage parlours, not feeling much like being around anyone. He wanted to make his money last, figuring it might be a while before he worked up the nerve to steal again. Or maybe he'd kill himself first.

Thoughts of suicide were becoming almost daily events, as Syrnyk regularly contemplated his role in life. Most days, he figured he didn't have one. Syrnyk briefly considered trying to pull off a bank heist in B.C., just to keep himself sharp, but didn't want to risk it in a major-league city he hardly knew. Vancouver was so intimidating, and Syrnyk felt like a small fish in a big pond.

Syrnyk did make one interesting purchase while on the west coast. His robbery spree had gotten him thinking about protection, believing it was only a matter of time before the guards started firing back. They were surely pissed at the fact he'd struck twice in a short time span, and thought some may adopt a "shoot first" approach. Syrnyk was especially worried about being shot in the back while he tried to flee. He found a specialty store in Vancouver that carried bullet-proof Kevlar vests, which were difficult to find in Winnipeg. Then, after nearly four months, Syrnyk decided it was time to come home.

● ● ● ● ● ●

At first, she was struck by his appearance – slim and pale, a slightly dishevelled look. When he spoke, she saw a man who was passive, meek and afraid to make eye contact. He spoke in a low, hushed voice, showing little emotion. Despite his apparent flaws and quirks, there was something about this obviously troubled man that left her wanting to know more.

Marlene Griffin (not her real name), single mother of three children, didn't exactly have a history of hitting the jackpot when it came to men. The father of her babies had split a long time ago, leaving Marlene to raise them on her own. A supportive family helped out whenever they could. She was working occasionally, taking whatever odd jobs she could to bring some money into the home. In mid-1999, after a chance meeting on a Winnipeg street, Marlene found herself in a deep discussion with a mysterious stranger named Michael Syrnyk.

Whores. That's what Syrnyk thought of most of the women he'd been with in his adult life, due largely to the circumstances he was meeting them in. Sex with him meant nothing, just another few bucks in their pocket before they moved on to the next nameless, faceless customer. It was a meat market; only Syrnyk was the buyer, not the server. Then he met Marlene.

She was different, so much more grounded and down-to-earth. And focused. She spoke about her children, the 10-year-old daughter, six-year-old son and three-year-old daughter, in a way that left Syrnyk thinking about his own childhood. She talked about her devotion to the kids, the hard knocks she'd received in life and her desire to build a better future for her children. Syrnyk was intrigued, but not enough to open up about his own life. He said little about his background, content to simply listen to Marlene's stories. He did offer to help Marlene out financially, using some of his money to get her back on her feet. Robin Hood, he wasn't. But Syrnyk felt a sense of pride in doing some good for a change.

••••••

September 2, 1999

The man on the phone was speaking quickly, a sense of urgency in his voice. The 911 operator listened intently. "I was just driving up to Wal-Mart. I saw a car parked behind some other vehicles at the east side of the building. I saw a person running from the car from the southeast corner of the building towards a Loomis truck that was parked in front of the doors. I thought he had a rifle. I saw him get close to the truck, still pointing the rifle!" the man said, his voice cracking with emotion. The dispatcher immediately triggered an audible alarm on the police radio communications system, alerting all officers that an urgent broadcast was coming. "Any units to respond to a report of a robbery of a Loomis armoured car which just occurred at the Unicity Shopping Centre at 3605 Portage Avenue. Suspect is believed to be armed with a rifle." Police officers from all areas of the city immediately began buzzing in to report they were en route. All units attending were reminded to use extreme caution.

The scene was chaotic when police arrived. Several witnesses described a sloppy getaway by the armed bandit, which included nearly knocking a woman over, tripping in a grassy knoll and fleeing the scene carrying two large bags stuffed with money. Two Loomis guards stood in front of the Wal-Mart and were visibly shaken, as were several bystanders who witnessed the dramatic 11:30 a.m. robbery.

Scott Delf identified himself to police as the guard who'd just been robbed. He estimated the loss was in the range of $100,000. Delf and his partner, Claude Vandale, described a day that was "business as usual" before the regular 11 a.m. Wal-Mart pickup, which was their fifteenth stop in a day which had only began two hours earlier. Vandale, the driver, stayed in the vehicle while Delf went inside the store for a delivery and pick-up. Delf believed he was back outside within four minutes. He returned to the truck, dodging an elderly shopper before opening up the rear door and tossing the money inside with some of the other pick-ups they'd already made. "That's when I heard footsteps running up behind," said Delf. He turned around and saw a "big black shotgun pointed at my chest." The man, who was wearing a white mask, was only two feet away.

The bandit ordered Delf to put his hands up and give him the bag. Delf raised his arms, but told the man the bag was already inside the truck. "Fuck you," the man said as he hopped up on the back and climbed inside. Delf told police the man seemed nervous as he ordered him to back up and get on his knees while still crawling inside the truck. Vandale picked up the story from there. The driver told police he heard some "muffled voices" coming from outside which drew his attention. "I couldn't make out what was being said. I turned around and looked through the window that looks into the back of the truck. I saw a person in the back of the van crouched down. I knew it wasn't Scott and at that point I realized we were being robbed," said Vandale. In a desperate move, Vandale said he threw the vehicle into drive and hit the gas pedal. He assumed the robber was still inside. Vandale also activated an audible siren. He drove about 75 yards before stopping, turning around and seeing the man was no longer in the back. The bandit had jumped out of the moving vehicle, holding two bags. He ran directly past Delf and towards a running vehicle that was parked at a stop sign, facing oncoming traffic. The suspect jumped inside and drove away.

A small but determined group of witnesses were running after the fleeing car, trying to get close enough to obtain the licence plate. "I was still in the parking lot when I noticed a beige car coming around the back side of Unicity towards me. To me, he was going pretty fast. As he took the corner towards the embankment he almost hit the embankment. He was going fast," said a woman who watched the action unfold seconds after leaving nearby Shopper's Drug Mart in the mall. "Then he stopped the car and jumped out carrying two bags. He ran over the embankment, going west. As he got to the top he almost ran into a woman." That woman was able to give police another small piece of the puzzle, describing how the man tripped and fell a couple times while running through a grassy knoll with his loot. The bandit then ran across a nearby street and got into a second parked vehicle, quickly driving away. She could only describe it as a "newer white car". Nobody was able to get a licence plate.

The suspect descriptions varied significantly from witness to witness. The woman who was nearly run over figured he was barely over 5'0, with a well-kept black beard and likely about 20 years old. Delf and Vandale described their attacker as stocky, perhaps over 200 pounds with a heavy build. They estimated he was about 5'8. Delf thought he saw a bushy grey and black moustache under the mask. Several other witnesses also described dark facial hair. Vandale distinctly remembered the red and black parka the man wore, an immediate trigger for major crime detectives looking to establish a link with the other armoured car robberies. Not that there was really any doubt.

Police recovered the first getaway car, a 1993 Plymouth Acclaim, just behind the mall. As usual, few clues were left behind. The only conclusion to draw was that either the robber or the people he'd stolen the car from didn't care much for cleanliness. Among the items found inside were two tennis balls, tan leather gloves, a crushed Kleenex box, a can of cherry mist air freshener, a pair of grey wool socks, a Famous Players drink cup, package of Excel gum, Robin's Donuts paper bag and a McDonald's drink cup and lid. Police tested every item for fingerprints with negative results. Same went for the punched steering column and the country music tape inside the stereo. One interesting item found in the vehicle was a *Winnipeg Sun* newspaper, dated August 31. Since the car had been stolen on August 29, it appeared the bandit bought the paper. Police were intrigued by the fact their man might be following the local news. Perhaps he was feeding off the attention his crimes were getting him?

Police went through the usual motions – notifying fellow officers working at the Winnipeg International Airport to be on the lookout for anything suspicious and putting an informal alert to Canada Customs officials at the Manitoba-North Dakota border. Police also canvassed several nearby homes and businesses, along with Winnipeg Transit drivers who may have been on scene at the time. There were no reports of anything unusual. The search would continue.

• • • • • •

It had been too tempting to resist. A near nine-month layoff had been too much for Syrnyk, who actually felt himself missing – actually craving – the adrenaline rush which came with the intricate planning and execution of a successful crime. He found his target easily, picking a busy retail outlet close to the outskirts of town. The west Portage Avenue location, not far from the Perimeter Highway that surrounded Winnipeg, ensured two things. First, police had quite a distance to travel before they could flood the area, giving Syrnyk precious getaway time. Second, he could always use the Perimeter Highway for a high-speed escape if necessary. Syrnyk had spent about 10 days following the Loomis guards on their route, learning every detail about every stop. As usual, it was overkill, but Syrnyk didn't mind. He actually loved the thrill of the chase, the feeling he was in control. The preparation work had clearly paid off, as the Wal-Mart heist went rather flawlessly. Having to jump from the back of the fleeing Loomis vehicle had offered an improvisational rush. And Syrnyk felt like he'd found a King's ransom when he opened the bags to find $100,000. It was more money they'd he'd ever seen in his life, two years of salary for the average working stiff. Well, the joke was on them. Syrnyk had made the money in half a day's work.

CHAPTER **9**

The news had rocked the Syrnyk family to its core – Virgina Syrnyk was dying of cancer. The disease was ravaging her ovaries, and doctors feared they could only prolong the inevitable for so long. Virginia had begun making plans for her death, including updating her will. With her marriage already in shambles, it didn't come as a major surprise that there was no reference to her husband in the legal documents.

His mother's cancer was a wake-up call for Michael Syrnyk, who had grown further apart from his parents in recent years as he embarked on his new career. Devastated by the news, Syrnyk began spending more time with his ailing mother, who had been living alone in their St. James home. Although there was some bitterness about a childhood that seemed lost, Syrnyk viewed his mother largely as a victim and felt they shared a deep, albeit unspoken, bond. He decided to move back in with his mother, to be there for her during her final days.

Syrnyk credited his mother for his sensitive side, one that included an unconditional love for animals. He could relate to all creatures big and small, from his childhood days of owning a hamster to the more recent years spent with Odin. Looking back, it was his mother's affection for all things furry and four-legged which Syrnyk recalled often leading to conflict in his parents' marriage. His father was an avid hunter, who would try to convince Syrnyk to come with him. He always balked, a position strongly supported by his mother. Syrnyk hated the idea of slaughtering an innocent animal, and could never understand or justify what his father did. It seemed cruel and unnecessary.

Brent Syrnyk and his fiancé, Sheri, thought of Syrnyk as the "champion of the underdog". Sheri's feelings were cemented by an incident at the Syrnyk summer cottage grounds in Bissett, in which Syrnyk saved the life of her old dog. Sandy's best years were long behind her, the old mutt nearly 18 years old and struggling to see or hear. That explained why the lovable pooch had snagged a fishhook in her throat while trying to bite what she likely thought was a minnow. Syrnyk wasted no time, grabbing a gagging Sandy and prying open her jaw. He reached his hands into her throat, carefully jiggling the hook until it broke free of its grip and came loose. The old girl just went on with her life as if nothing had happened, but Sheri was forever grateful for what Syrnyk had done. "I just fell in love with her. She has such a good spirit. She just keeps getting back up and back up," Syrnyk often told Sheri. From that day forward, Sandy always

112

seemed to remember what Syrnyk did for her, wagging her tail and showing as much enthusiasm as she could at her age whenever he walked into the room.

Syrnyk also had a soft spot for single mothers, given his own parents' difficulties and his mother largely raising the two boys on her own. One recent winter, Brent was expecting Syrnyk over for a visit and grew concerned when he was late. He called his brother, who was actually waiting at an inner-city bus stop with a young single mother. Syrnyk had been driving to Brent's when he saw the woman standing next to a baby carriage, trying to shelter herself and the child from the cold air and blowing snow. Not wanting to scare her by offering the woman a ride, Syrnyk elected to call the woman a cab and then pay for it when it arrived, rather than leave her waiting for a bus which was surely delayed by the bad weather. It was images such as this, burned in Syrnyk's deeply troubled head, which had given him fits while robbing the banks and seeing the frightened faces of young mothers.

• • • • • •

September 10, 1999

Syrnyk was doing something that came very naturally to him – running. Only today it was with a shotgun in his hands. Syrnyk decided it was time to upgrade his weapon collection, and chose the S.I.R. gun store as the place to do it. He was falling in love with guns, of all shapes and sizes, and felt his current supply was inadequate. That could easily be rectified. Shortly after 8:30 p.m., a masked Syrnyk stormed into the popular Winnipeg business, making a beeline for the gun counter. His goal today was to be in and out within a minute – just like the Stopwatch Gang. Syrnyk said nothing to the handful of staff and customers inside the store, figuring his weapon and brisk pace were sending a strong enough message. One hand was on the pistol grip, while the other was in a menacing position halfway up the forearm of the black stock. He held the shotgun tightly against his chest. Syrnyk reached the counter, pushing open the swinging gate to get in behind. A middle-aged man

working the counter was actually holding a shotgun, which he had been in the process of showing to a customer. Wisely – and to Syrnyk's relief – the man put the gun down on the counter and backed away several steps. Syrnyk went to the gun rack against the wall, grabbing all three mini-14 rifles he could see. He recognized the unique gun instantly, which was smaller than the normal long gun and capable of shooting a high velocity, military-style ammunition. As he turned to flee, one of the rifles fell from his hands to the ground. Syrnyk swore to himself, angry he had messed up. His anger intensified seconds later when, after scooping up the gun, he tripped over the swinging gate while trying to crawl over it. Those damn gates! How many times would this happen before he learned? Syrnyk regained his balance, hung on to the weapons and continued his run out the door. Total robbery time had been close to a minute, but Syrnyk felt more humiliated than heroic.

More guns in the hands of a potential maniac. Winnipeg police were stumped to solve the latest weapons haul in the city. Links to the unsolved bank and armoured car heists couldn't be ruled out, and the description of the suspect in the S.I.R. incident suggested the same man might be involved. Police also wondered if the culprit could be responsible for the August 1994 break-in and theft of guns at the same S.I.R. store, or the January 1998 Wal-Mart theft. The suspect description in this latest incident was also similar to the one provided by witnesses to the October 1998 Farmer's Supply hold-up. Police shuddered at the kind of arsenal their mystery man must possess if behind all four robberies. And did the fact he appeared to be loading up again suggest another attack was imminent?

• • • • • •

Kevlar is a criminal's best friend. At least, that's the motto Syrnyk was adopting as he prepared to gear up for another busy holiday season. Although he was the proud owner of one bullet proof vest, Syrnyk no longer felt like that was sufficient. Police, and especially armoured car guards, were likely preparing for another incident and would surely be better prepared. So Syrnyk would ensure he was also on top of his game. He had read in various books and publications about the concept of full body armour, and Syrnyk had a vision to turn himself into a sort of Robo-Robber. The concept was simple – get another vest or two and wrap his body in a Kevlar apron, protecting him from neck to toe. Syrnyk knew just the place to kick-start his plan.

December 17, 1999

"Ding Dong." The familiar door enunciator signalled the arrival of a late evening customer inside The Spy Shop, a popular downtown Winnipeg business filled with the latest electronic gadgetry. Want to spy on your nanny? Figure your husband to be a cheating louse and need to bug the telephone? The Spy Shop was the place to come. Dan Hawkins and one of his employees were working together this night, tending to some paperwork in the back office. They got up from a desk and began walking towards the showroom to greet their customer. But instead of seeing a smiling face, Hawkins and the employee saw the back of a man who appeared to be carrying one of the store's bullet proof vests. Only this customer was masked and appeared to be leaving the store. "Hey, what are you doing?" asked Hawkins. The man turned around. In his hands was a sawed-off, pump action shotgun.

Hawkins saw the gunman was carrying four other vests, which were fakes. He and his employee immediately dove for cover, hitting the ground behind the counter. They could hear footsteps as the man continued out the door and onto Edmonton Street. The door closed automatically behind him. A shaken Hawkins reached for the phone to dial 911.

Back home, Syrnyk felt more prepared then ever. A little manipulation here and there, and he had cleverly outfitted himself with full body-armour. His sense of confidence was extremely high as he prepared to make Christmas 1999 a memorable occasion.

Winnipeg Free Press – December 18, 1999

A thief armed with a shotgun and delusions of invincibility made off with five bullet-proof vests from the city's premiere shop for security gadgets last night – too bad four of them were dummies. "I put the props out because I have to," Dan Hawkins, owner of the Spy Shop on Edmonton Street, said not long after the 7:30 p.m. robbery, the second one targeting bullet-proof vests at his shop in six weeks. The Kevlar vests retail for $800 or more and Hawkins said he only sells to people working legitimate security jobs. "Hopefully he says 'Try this one out,'" he said of the robber and his cache of fake vests. Hawkins has installed a "fog machine" that instantly fills the shop with smoke if a window is broken during a break-in. But this time he was hit while the store was still open.

• • • • • •

The $100,000 September robbery had gone to Syrnyk's head, prompting him to make plans for a return engagement. Only this time, he was going to have a little help. A man he'd met while in Vancouver, a drifter with a checkered past, had breezed into town and looked Syrnyk up. Syrnyk had told Jim very little about his own life, not wanting to spill his secrets to a stranger. But the thought of having someone tag alone was becoming increasingly appealing to Syrnyk, who often daydreamed about forming his own Stopwatch Gang. He would be leader, of course. But the biggest obstacle was finding someone who he was not only comfortable being around, but could also trust with his life. Perhaps Jim could be that man? With the West Coast visitor in town, Syrnyk suggested they visit Unicity Mall.

December 23, 1999

The sight of two masked men running through the parking lot – one carrying a sawed-off shotgun – stopped several would-be customers in their tracks. It was 11:15 a.m., prompting some people to wonder if what they were witnessing could even be real. Yet it was real, and thankfully a few concerned witnesses promptly picked up their cellular phones and dialled 911. The call was becoming frighteningly familiar to Winnipeg police – an apparent robbery in progress. Once again, the combustible combination of guns and crowded shopping mall parking lots was a major worry as police sped towards the scene.

Syrnyk ran to the rear door of the Loomis truck while Jim tried grabbing a side door. The driver sat inside, staring straight ahead. His partner was inside the mall. Syrnyk decided not to confront the guard this time, figuring he'd make an easy snatch and grab from the back of the truck. He hadn't counted on the doors being locked. But they were. Syrnyk admitted defeat on the spot. "Let's go," he screamed to Jim. The pair ran to a waiting van, which they'd left running for their getaway. Syrnyk drove away empty-handed.

The Loomis guard returned to the vehicle, joining his partner who was waiting inside. The employees slowly pulled away from the mall. To their surprise, Winnipeg police flooded the parking lot, waving them down. Witnesses were describing the aborted robbery attempt of their truck. The Loomis employees were shocked, having been completely oblivious to the entire debacle.

Syrnyk was furious with himself on so many levels. How could he have been so foolish? Any momentum he was carrying from the September robbery had been dashed in a heartbeat, the decision to bring in a partner and to try and pounce on the unsuspecting armoured car driver had failed miserably. Syrnyk decided to go back to his original game plan of working alone and being patient and prepared. He drowned his sorrows in a sea of alcohol and marijuana, and then planned his next move. He wasn't going to wait very long.

• • • • • •

Christmas Eve, 1999

Dale Lagimodiere had a nervous feeling as he came to work. Like everyone in his profession, the Loomis guard heard about the previous day's attempted hold-up, and there were fears the frustrated bandit or bandits would try and strike again. Instead of a festive, holiday spirit, Lagimodiere and his two partners were on edge and just wanted to safely make it through their shift.

Just after noon, the men pulled into the parking lot of the Wal-Mart store on Kenaston Boulevard and McGillivray Road. The big box retailer had been raking in the cash during a lucrative Christmas shopping season, and Lagimodiere and a fellow guard were about to make a major cash pickup. Yet another cause for concern. Lagimodiere and his partner took an extra few seconds to check their surroundings before leaving the vehicle. Nothing unusual. After parking near the store, Lagimodiere got out alone for a closer look. It was his job to ensure the scene was safe for his partner. Lagimodiere gave the other the green light and the man joined him outside the vehicle. The third Loomis guard stayed behind the wheel. Lagimodiere and his partner walked inside, carrying an empty bag, and loaded several thousand dollars while standing in a protected "cash cage" in Wal-Mart. Once filled, the men prepared to leave. Their eyes nervously darted back and forth, searching the store for any sign of trouble. Nothing. Lagimodiere walked out the front doors first, with his partner close behind carrying the money bag. Lagimodiere was confident the scene was secure, telling his partner to continue walking. He stopped near a bicycle rack, guarding his partner while he got inside the truck with the cash. His partner shut the door and locked it. Lagimodiere began moving towards the passenger door. He was a few metres away when the Yuletide Bandit darted out from the corner of the store, heading straight for him and the truck.

Syrnyk knew he'd waited too long to pounce. He was trying to make up the lost time with a spirited run, but already had a sense of dread. Syrnyk went straight for the side door of the truck, the one he'd just watched get closed, and began pounding on it with his left hand. The other hand was holding a Glock pistol, pointing directly at the Loomis guard. "Open the fucking door!" Syrnyk shouted.

Lagimodiere was terrified, but knew any misstep could cost him his life. He raised his hands slowly in the air, away from his gun that was still in the holster around his waist. There had been no chance to pull it out. Lagimodiere's eyes were trained on the masked gunman, who briefly turned away to concentrate on the locked door. Lagimodiere took these precious seconds to back away along the bicycle rack, hoping to take cover somewhere. With a more comfortable distance between them, Lagimodiere did the unthinkable. He pulled out his gun.

"Go fuck yourself," Syrnyk screamed, the sight of the guard drawing his weapon sending a jolt through his body. "Put it down," the man shouted back. The move triggered an instant reaction in Syrnyk. He squeezed the trigger. Syrnyk backed up, trying to take cover behind the truck. He fired another shot. The guard ducked down, behind the bike rack. Syrnyk heard another crack of gunfire, knowing this one hadn't come from his gun. He was under siege. Syrnyk quickly fired two more shots in return.

Sixteen-year-old Jason, his young sister and their father had gone to the mall today to do some last-minute Christmas shopping for Mom. The family was just about to enter Wal-Mart when the robbery went down. The scene was surreal. The father tried to get his children out of harms way as they were standing in front of a vending machine directly behind where the Loomis guard had taken cover. "Turn around and run," the man told his kids. Jason and his sister did as told, heading around the corner of the store. But the bullets started flying as they fled. Jason felt something hit his elbow, followed immediately by a tiny black object falling to the ground beside him. He assumed it was dirt or mud he'd kicked up while running.

Lagimodiere had a seemingly perfect view of the bandit, aiming his gun directly through one of the tires he was kneeling behind. He was aiming right for the man's chest. He was shooting to kill. The robber seemed to stumble, and Lagimodiere at first thought he'd hit him. "Shots fired, shots fired!" the Loomis driver bellowed into his two-way radio. With his gun in one hand, he had called in to their dispatcher at the first sight of the bandit, telling them to call police immediately. The driver had remained inside the vehicle, per company policy, praying the police would arrive quickly.

Syrnyk felt the breeze as the bullet whizzed by his head, which was about the only part of his body not covered in armour. He hit the ground, rolling around and doing a crab crawl on the snow-packed pavement. Syrnyk didn't hear any more shots, so he jumped up and began running, partially covered by the truck. He made an angled line towards the rear parking lot, where his getaway car was parked. He was empty-handed, again, but this was no longer about money. It was about survival.

With the bandit quickly moving out of sight, Lagimodiere's partner got out of the truck and joined him. The driver stayed behind the wheel, providing important details to the dispatcher. The driver could see a crowd was quickly forming in the parking lot, which only increased the potential for more violence. He activated the public address system inside the Loomis truck. "Please, everyone, get back inside the store," the driver announced in a commanding voice. Most people quickly complied, while a handful of gawkers stayed outside for a closer look at the chaos.

Lagimodiere's partner wanted to pursue the robber, but Lagimodiere told him to stop and use his brain. They didn't know what they might be getting into, and clearly the bandit wasn't afraid to use his weapon. The guards saw a white car peel out of the parking lot moments later. As they walked back to their truck, Lagimodiere felt his right leg go numb. He looked down and saw a bullet hole in his pants. Then he saw the blood. He had been shot.

Police swarmed the scene, with some officers searching the parking lot and surrounding area and others heading directly to the guards and other witnesses. An ambulance was called for Lagimodiere, who showed officers the tear in his pants and the wound on his right calf. It didn't look too serious, fortunately, but police wanted Lagimodiere to go to the hospital. Meanwhile, other officers tracked down the man and children who were caught in the crossfire. The family was still standing beside the store. Police noticed the teenaged boy, Jason, was shaking like a leaf. The young boy described the shooting, and the strange sensation of something hitting his elbow and a mysterious black object falling to the ground. Police immediately went for Jason's jacket, removing it for a closer look. It didn't take long for them to find the bullet hole in his sleeve.

CHAPTER 10

Michael Syrnyk paced the floor, his twitching hand clutching a half-smoked marijuana joint. He brought the reefer to his lips and sucked deeply. There was much going through his head on this cold January day, and none of it was good. The holidays had been a disaster, two failed Christmas robberies eating away at his very fibre, causing Syrnyk to second-guess everything he'd accomplished up to this point. It wasn't about the money, as Syrnyk still had plenty left from the big fall heist. His wallet was full. But his confidence was empty. *I am such a piece of shit*, Syrnyk thought to himself. I can't do this anymore.

Syrnyk could still feel the bullet speeding by his head, a millisecond in time he'd frozen forever. At first, the near-death experience had scared him. But in the days that followed, he found himself actually wishing it had hit him. He was angry he was still alive.

Syrnyk was again fighting his own conscience, something he attributed to the pot. It was a truth serum, making him soft to the point he was being haunted by the people he could have killed. He remembered seeing some young kids in the parking lot, and wondered how the chaos had looked to them. A small part of him hoped they would be okay, recalling his own teenaged years and how messed up his mind was. He hoped they would make out better in life.

● ● ● ● ● ●

The shooting of a 16-year-old innocent bystander was enough to make even the most hardened, emotionless cop sit up and take notice. Major crime detectives who interviewed Jason would never forget the frightened look on his face when they discovered the bullet fragment lodged in his jacket. "I was going into Wal-Mart with my dad and sister to shop for some last-minute Christmas gifts. I was sort of standing behind my dad. I saw a guy standing by the Loomis truck. I didn't really get a good look at him. Then my dad said 'turn around and run'," Jason told the officers in his statement. "As soon as my dad said that I knew there was something wrong. I ran and went around the corner. I remember the guy yelling 'open the door'. As I was running away I heard some shots and felt something hit my elbow." The words, written by a teenaged boy, were chilling. Police knew that a few inches to the side, or higher, and Jason could have been killed. Same goes for the other dozen witnesses who gave statements to police. Police offered the distraught family access to their victims services program and follow-up counselling if needed, knowing the boy's worst days could still be ahead as the realization of what happened to him – and what could have happened – really sunk in.

Dale Lagimodiere had a physical scar to go with the emotional one he was bearing. Fortunately, the bandit's bullet had just caused a minor flesh wound to his leg, which in time would fully heal. The shooting of the Loomis guard was the most dramatic wake-up call to date for all security personnel across the city, which realized what a cold, calculating psychopath they were dealing with. Clearly, the gunman wouldn't think twice about taking them down. While some guards were shaken, others were downright angry and vowed to be more vigilant. Their lives were at stake. Winnipeg police knew they had a potential powder keg on their hands, with guards more likely to open or return fire at the first sight of the masked robber. Jason was living proof of how dangerous the situation had become.

Unfortunately, police were no closer to finding the culprit, who was clearly getting more brazen with each passing crime. Although plenty of people had seen him, no witnesses were able to offer much more than the same type of vague, general description police had been getting for the past few years. Police did recover the stolen getaway car, but their man was long gone and had left no clues behind. Lagimodiere thought there was a chance he could have hit the man in the shootout, but police found no blood inside the car to suggest the robber was injured. And while no money was taken during the robbery, that was actually cause for major concern – it likely wouldn't be long before the Yuletide Bandit tried to strike again.

• • • • • •

The psychedelic lights pumped in rhythm to the electronic music as dry ice created a smokescreen on the dance floor. A mass of people, most in their late teens and twenties, contorted their bodies to the pounding beat. This was sensory overload. In the back of the warehouse, soaking up this bizarre scene stood Michael Syrnyk.

He had come here, reluctantly, at the urging of a wild, doe-eyed girl he'd met days earlier at a massage parlour. The sex had been frisky, and freaky, and there was something about her that had intrigued him. Kim had encouraged Syrnyk to get out of his self-imposed shell, offering him a colourful little pill she said would make it much easier. Syrnyk at first resisted, but eventually gave in during a moment of weakness. He figured there was nothing left to lose in his miserable life.

It didn't take long to feel the change. Syrnyk had read plenty about Ecstasy, the popular mood altering designer pill that had only recently come onto the drug scene in Winnipeg. Almost immediately, Syrnyk felt a sense of confidence and awakening. With the drug in his system, Syrnyk actually felt comfortable with the prospect of going with Kim to a crowded club scene.

The Yuletide Bandit

"Little Sis" – that's what Syrnyk took to calling Kim, who in turn responded by calling him "Big Brother." As the winter began to melt away, Syrnyk was spending much of his time with Little Sis, who had opened up an exciting new world to him. Marlene Griffin had done the same months earlier, but Syrnyk had pulled back from that family scene, finding it too difficult to fit in. He was also avoiding his own family. Little Sis, though, was downright crazy, a party girl who wasn't afraid to let loose. Syrnyk found himself laughing more than he had in years, as Kim took him from one social event to another. Ecstasy had made interacting with others easy, rather than painful, and Syrnyk actually looked forward to getting out. He no longer felt ashamed and trapped by his own fears and anxiety, the drugs helping to mask the pain of his own mother's failing health. He felt alive.

It wasn't long before Syrnyk was expanding his drug repertoire, as Little Sis introduced him to a buffet of new chemicals. Magic mushrooms and LSD became regular drugs of choice, with Syrnyk experimenting several times a week. His days became a haze of partying, sex and drugs. Syrnyk was quickly making friends, thanks to a seemingly endless flow of money that allowed him to treat everyone to whatever they pleased. He was giving away as much, if not more, than he was using. Syrnyk figured it was working so well for him, so why not spread the wealth?

For the first time since the botched Christmas robberies, Syrnyk's shattered confidence had been repaired. His mind began drifting to thoughts of his next big strike. As the weeks passed by quickly, Syrnyk was also having thoughts of bringing a partner into the mix – Little Sis. She certainly was daring enough to do it, and Syrnyk felt like he could definitely trust her. The prospect of a Bonnie and Clyde relationship was intriguing. The botched Christmas robbery with his Vancouver acquaintance had soured him on the idea of a tag-team, but the shopping mall shootout the following day was proof he could probably use some help. Besides, he was actually enjoying the company of others and felt more comfortable than ever at the prospect of having a partner. Syrnyk hadn't told Little Sis much about his lifestyle, keeping his criminal background a secret for fear it would be accidentally spilled to others during a drugged-out night of partying. He vowed to wait a bit longer to see how things develop before making a final decision.

••••••

At first, the thought of putting an animal tranquilizer into his body scared the hell out of Syrnyk. He had read a little about ketamine, with some literature suggesting it gives users a near-death experience. Syrnyk already knew what that felt like, but was talked into trying the drug by a persuasive Little Sis. She had used it, and promised him the experience of a lifetime. She was right. Syrnyk went on a tortuous spiritual journey, experiencing psychosis and paranoia to extremes he'd never felt before.

The one drug Syrnyk swore off was cocaine. Little Sis was a user, and was trying to get him to try it. Syrnyk knew enough about coke to be worried, well aware that it was highly addictive and dangerous. This was one road he refused to go down. Eventually, his resistance would drive him and Little Sis apart. She was doing coke regularly, and would get angry that Syrnyk wouldn't join her. Little Sis would go on day-long binges, and Syrnyk hated what he saw. Her entire demeanour and attitude would change, the little hellcat he loved so much transforming into a strung-out, aggressive junkie right before his eyes.

As spring arrived, Syrnyk made the difficult choice to walk away from the girl who'd given him so much in just a few short weeks. He didn't think it was healthy to stay together, and felt it was best to get away from her and the lifestyle she was living. It was a painful decision, but one he figured was for the best. She was too much of a mess to be his Bonnie.

• • • • • •

May 12, 2000

Syrnyk wasn't fooling around this time. Although somewhat nervous, he'd spent a couple weeks planning his next move out to ensure nothing would go wrong. He had taken the time to scout out the route and get to know his targets, at least from a distance. This was an important step for Syrnyk. He wouldn't tolerate failure for a third straight time.

Syrnyk pulled into the parking lot of the Safeway store on Mountain Avenue, driving a white Jeep he'd just stolen. He sat inside the running vehicle, his gear on the seat beside him, waiting for the Loomis truck to arrive. Syrnyk was expecting a three person crew today – a male and female guard who would leave the truck, and a man who would remain behind the wheel. He'd thought about the fact he was back to targeting a woman, but Syrnyk didn't feel the same discomfort as he had during the latter stages of the bank hold-ups. This was different. She was trained, armed, and likely ready for anything, given the recent climate in Winnipeg. Besides, Syrnyk was planning for this to go smoothly. He would draw his gun, of course, but hoped not to have to use it. But how the guards, already on edge, would respond was the great unknown.

The truck pulled into the crowded lot, right on schedule, and took its position near the main front entrance to the store. The female guard and her male partner exited slowly, taking a long look around. Syrnyk was still inside his vehicle, many metres away. The guards eventually moved forward and disappeared into the store. Syrnyk prepared to move as well. He knew they wouldn't be long. He slipped on his balaclava, grabbed his gun and checked to make sure his full-body Kevlar vest was secure. He sprinted to an alcove just beside the entrance. He was ready to pounce.

The Loomis driver was sitting behind the wheel of the truck when the sight of a man running by caught his attention. The first thing he noticed was the black mask. Then he saw the shotgun. Seconds later as his co-workers walked out of the grocery store, loaded money bag in hand. He knew they were in serious trouble. The driver leaned on his horn, screaming and pointing at his two partners as the masked man darted from around the corner.

"Drop the fucking money, you fucking asshole," Syrnyk shouted at the female guard. He was pointing his gun directly at the woman and her partner, who was standing several feet behind still in the doorway. She immediately put her hands in the air. But the man dropped to the ground in a crouch position, pulling out his gun and moving behind a magazine case. Syrnyk braced for the worst. The sound of a blaring car horn was also distracting him, putting an already fragile Syrnyk more on edge. Syrnyk was relieved when the woman quickly dropped the money bag to the ground. He reached down and picked it up, keeping his eyes and gun trained on the two guards. With money in hand, Syrnyk began running as fast as he could. He was expecting to hear gunshots, but none came his way. Syrnyk disappeared behind the building, headed for a stolen van he'd left waiting down the street.

The Loomis driver had alerted his dispatcher they were being robbed and police arrived quickly. It was still too late. The bandit had made a clean getaway, escaping with an estimated $18,000. Fortunately, the incident had gone rather smoothly and nobody was hurt. Police figured it was just a stroke of luck, and feared the next time they wouldn't be so lucky.

CHAPTER 11

Brent Syrnyk and his common law wife, Sheri, woke up in the early morning, knowing they had a full day ahead of them. As new homeowners, the couple had tried – and failed miserably – to re-sod their moss-filled front lawn. The new grass hadn't taken, quickly turning an ugly shade of brown the way a half-eaten apple responds when left out too long. So Brent had gone out the previous night, buying more sod for a second attempt. He was not looking forward to it. Brent got dressed and headed outside to begin the task at hand. He reached the front door, and was stopped dead in his tracks. His brother was standing in the yard. Beneath him was glorious green grass. Brent was astounded. Michael Syrnyk explained he had come by during the night, sometime around 2 a.m., and began digging up the yard himself. Using the fresh pile Brent had bought, Syrnyk spent the next four hours laying down nature's new carpet. It looked perfect, the seams hardly noticeable, the grass firm to the ground.

Syrnyk had always been a workhorse, never afraid to get his hands dirty. He was also deeply loyal, and valued all that Brent had done for him in their lives. When life was complicated and confusing – as it always seemed to be – Brent was the voice of calm and reason. Syrnyk hadn't listened to his brother's advice as much as he should, and knew he'd let both Brent and his family down. If only they knew how much.

Syrnyk quickly bonded with Brent's new love, and was thrilled that his brother had finally found happiness. Sheri was a wonderful woman with a warm heart, a big smile and an ear always willing to listen. In the spring of 2000, Syrnyk began spending more time with Brent and Sheri, both in their west Winnipeg home and during trips out to the property in Bissett where the ramshackle Syrnyk family cottage once stood. Now, it was just a plot of barren land, where they'd set up tents and stay the weekend. It was during these country excursions that Sheri and Brent really sensed just how troubled Syrnyk was. But getting him to open up was difficult, if not downright impossible. "What the hell can I do? I can't fit in. I can't be around people," Syrnyk would say to his brother whenever asked about any job prospects or future plans. Then he would change the topic, or just stop talking altogether. At the not so tender age of 30, Syrnyk had started smoking cigarettes, something he had always sworn off as a disgusting habit. "It makes me feel really sick, but I like it," Syrnyk would say. His bizarre answer only raised more questions.

Just as they did when they were younger, Syrnyk would occasionally disappear for hours, sometimes

The Yuletide Bandit

even a few days, taking only a handful of supplies with him into the woods. Syrnyk would pack some dates, nuts and packaged milk, sleeping under the stars by himself while Brent and Sheri returned to Winnipeg. Syrnyk felt most at peace when he was alone, and the period following the Safeway robbery was a most confusing time. He was spending increasingly long hours alone inside movie theatres or renting videos at home, burying himself in the fictional lives of others. Syrnyk was fascinated with the movie *Fight Club*, which was released a year earlier in theatres to almost universal applause from critics and audiences. Syrnyk related strongly to the lead character of Tyler Durden, who was portrayed in the movie by Hollywood mega-star Brad Pitt. The Durden character is drawn to another character not unlike Syrnyk – a sad, white-collar loner. Durden and the loner get into a friendly fight, which is seen by others and serves as the inspiration for the creation of a Fight Club, which goes underground and draws disillusioned and depraved young men to join. Syrnyk was living out his own Fight Club, using his feelings of isolation and loneliness to fuel an exciting and challenging idea. The only difference was Syrnyk was the lone member of his club.

Other recent movies were now serving as inspiration for Syrnyk, not unlike the effect *Apocalypse Now* and *Clockwork Orange* had on him during his younger years. *The Matrix*, a science-fiction thriller, was at the top of his list. Syrnyk was convinced the

Mike McIntyre

box-office smash had been made just for him. Once again, he identified with the main character, a dark and mysterious loner named Neo who embarks on a futuristic adventure filled with epic battles of good versus evil where the lines are often blurred. Syrnyk was also enjoying reading Sun Tzu's *Art of War*, an ancient Chinese classic that details principles of war and military strategy, as well as works on Zen Buddhism. In another life, in another time, Syrnyk pictured himself as a Buddhist, living a much happier existence then the one he had now.

Syrnyk felt like he was at a crossroads, an important point in his life that would ultimately decide his future. The last few months had been such a blur. Two botched robberies, a dramatic change in lifestyle, and now what? Not to mention his mother was slowly dying of cancer, the disease eating away at her body and soul as Syrnyk could only watch helplessly. Professionally, Syrnyk felt back on track with the Safeway robbery going down just as planned. Personally and emotionally, he was a bigger mess then ever. Syrnyk had reduced both his drug usage and trips to the massage parlours, preferring to lay low for a while. But he was having mixed thoughts about where he wanted to go from here. There was a part of him which wanted to get right back in the game, plan his next heist, and make it as big and ballsy as ever. Another part of him was saying, "chill out", take a breather, and re-assess where he was in life. Clearly, he was in too deep now to stop. Or was he?

The Yuletide Bandit

· · · · · ·

It was awkward, at first, meeting three innocent young faces who were so obviously attached to their mommy. Syrnyk said very little, allowing his friend Marlene Griffin to do most of the talking. The kids were little bundles of energy, and clearly didn't care about the emotional baggage Syrnyk was carrying. He found this refreshing, even uplifting.

Syrnyk began making regular trips to Marlene's house, not completely understanding why. All he knew was he felt good during these visits, with a sense of optimism he hadn't experienced in some time, if ever. It had been nearly a year since he met Marlene, and yet their initial friendship had stalled and sputtered while Syrnyk focused on what he believed were more important things in his life. Now, however, Syrnyk actually wanted to spend time with this woman who always seemed to be able to put a smile on his face. And the little ones could brighten even the darkest of days. Syrnyk would get down on the floor, roll up his sleeves and play with the kids as if he were one himself. They would laugh, sing and make funny faces. A strong bond was quickly formed, with Syrnyk filling an obvious void left in the children's lives since their father had walked out. In return, the kids were filling a void in Syrnyk life.

In quieter times, once the little ones were tucked into bed, Syrnyk and Marlene would engage in lengthy conversations, mostly about their pasts. Syrnyk had always glossed over much of his, painting a fairly generic picture of a happy home, normal childhood and regular Joe kind of lifestyle. But as the weeks wore on and Syrnyk became more comfortable opening up to Marlene, he began to break down his outer wall and give her a glimpse into his tortured existence. Syrnyk was initially careful with what he said, not wanting to give away too much. But he found the words flowed easier then he expected, likely because Marlene was so understanding. She didn't judge, but simply listened. The couple talked, they cried, they hugged. The conversations would spill over for hours, even days. Eventually, the talks began leading to a kiss. And a trip to the bedroom.

A happy home filled with laughing children was no place for the tools of a cold-blooded criminal. So, with his surprising and unexpected friendship with Marlene blossoming into something more, Syrnyk took an important step to separate the two very different lives he was now leading. He signed a contract with an inner-city storage compound, allowing him to rent a private locker. The agreement simply stated he was allowed to store "personal items". For Syrnyk, that meant his bullet proof vest, his police scanner and earpiece, some break-in tools, nearly 1,000 rounds of ammunition and the guns he hadn't tossed into the river. They were out of sight, but definitely not out of mind.

Step dad. Syrnyk stopped in his tracks the first time Marlene's children called him this.

The Yuletide Bandit

It was a major step, one that Syrnyk didn't think he was ready to take. After all, he often felt like he was just one of the kids, struggling to fit into their world which seemed so simple yet rewarding. Syrnyk was hardly a role model, definitely not someone they should look up to. Yet to the children, he was someone they clearly adored. It all just seemed too much, too fast. Syrnyk had no idea why Marlene and her children cared so deeply. He felt he didn't deserve their love, or even their attention. Yet Marlene, now fully aware of the demons he was battling, had proclaimed her love for him. Syrnyk admired her strength and commitment to her family. But it wasn't a commitment he was ready to make. Syrnyk still felt a strong pull towards a life of chaos, and wasn't ready to let it go despite Marlene's pleas. He began to pull back from her and the children, a painful decision but one he felt necessary. And he began planning for another busy holiday season.

CHAPTER 12

December 12, 2000

There was no escaping the bitter reality – even for Winnipeg in December, it was bloody cold. People who began their day at 7 a.m. awoke to a -30 temperature, combined with a stiff north wind that made it feel more like -41 Celsius. The bleak forecast provided little hope of improvement throughout the day. The temperature was still dropping by the time hundreds of holiday-weary shoppers began congregating at the city's busiest mall around mid-morning. Finding a parking spot was tougher than tracking down a Tickle-Me Elmo.

And most shoppers would probably agree a half-kilometre hike from their car to the nearest mall entrance was far worse than putting up with never-ending store line-ups or that obnoxious, overbearing Christmas Muzak. But for 50 hustling, bustling customers who happened to be using the south mall entrance just after noon on this day, something far more dramatic than a slap in the face by the frigid arctic air was about to hit them.

Mike McIntyre

• • • • • •

It had been seven long months, to the day in fact, since Michael Syrnyk had faced his fears. Short on money, Syrnyk had been watching the calendar the way a wide-eyed young child would, counting down the days until the busy Christmas season had cash registers ringing. Syrnyk wasn't going to wait for the presents to come to him. He knew where to find them, and how to get them. This year, his target was Polo Park Shopping Mall, barely a stone's throw from the home he was living at with his dying mother.

The city's most popular shopping centre, Polo Park boasts more than 200 shops and services, from one-of-a-kind specialty boutiques to national chain and department stores. The mall is an important stop for every serious holiday shopper in Winnipeg, and Syrnyk, of course, knew this. There was major money flowing through the tills every second, like blood through a vein, keeping the local economy pumping. The thought also sent Syrnyk's heart racing. He'd spent the last couple of weeks standing in the parking lot of Polo Park, watching quietly behind snow banks and through exhaust fog as two armoured car guards went about their regular routine of picking up deposits and delivering cash, their bags always bursting. Syrnyk knew they might be expecting him, given his previous holiday heists. But it didn't matter. He was better prepared, better equipped than they could have ever imagined. In the past day, Syrnyk had discreetly stolen three cars, a trade at which he was becoming an expert. He cleverly positioned the cars at various checkpoints around the city. Polo Park was going to go smoothly. The Yuletide Bandit would have a Merry Christmas, indeed.

• • • • • •

Securicor driver Blake Kendall was always nervous handling large sums of money, especially given the recent crime climate in Winnipeg. He was painfully aware of the time of the year, and the potential for violence. The 10-year armoured car veteran had gone seven years on the job without hearing of a single armoured car heist in the city. Now, they seemed to be routine, almost expected. Kendall had read the internal company memos, heard the nervous chatter and gossip amongst co-workers, and always planned for the worst. Yet he still had a job to do. Kendall's first task at Polo Park today – possibly the most risky – had gone smoothly. Within a few minutes, he had personally delivered $100,000 cash to the Safeway store inside the mall, located on the eastern side of the building. Kendall returned to his truck and moved it to the south entrance, parking just outside the CIBC bank. A second guard, Ryan Krueger, remained inside the vehicle at all times as per company policy. He had been told this four weeks ago, when he first started working for Loomis. There had been talk of permanently adding a third guard to all Loomis runs instead of just select ones because it was approaching

Christmas and the robbery risk was increasing. But on this day, it was just Kendall and Krueger.

It was nearly noon when Kendall left the truck and dropped off some more cash inside the bank. In return, he was given a bag containing $1,100. Kendall was to deliver it to the bank's head office in Winnipeg later that afternoon. Kendall moved on, now to the Manitoba Telecom Services branch inside the mall. The MTS employees gave him a disposable white bag containing $61,000 in cash and cheques. This was considered a major pick-up. Kendall once again had a nervous feeling carrying so much cash as he headed straight for the exit doors, to his truck waiting outside. He got about 15 feet outside the doors, just next to some small tree planters, when he saw the man in the black balaclava.

"Drop it!" Syrnyk shouted at his prey. Wearing a red and black three-quarter length winter coat, Syrnyk had been waiting anxiously for this moment, sitting outside near the hexagonal glass atrium housing the stairs leading up to Moxie's family restaurant. He'd been trying to look discreet and cool, but this did not come easy, nor naturally, to a man with Syrnyk's erratic personality. Syrnyk pounced as soon as he saw the guard. He began running towards the guard, his gun drawn. If Syrnyk were competing in the 100-metre dash, it probably would have been ruled a false start on the grounds he left the blocks too early. But Syrnyk was battling nerves and this was no time to second-guess. "Just give it up, just give it up," he bellowed, moving now within about 20 feet of his target. Syrnyk peered through his eyeholes and saw the look of fear that had become so common in recent years. He knew he was in control. As he approached the guard, winter suddenly took its toll in a most cruel and humiliating way – Syrnyk's feet gave out on the icy pavement and he fell flat on his back.

Looking up at the guard, Syrnyk reacted instinctively, squeezing the trigger of his Browning nine-millimetre handgun. Inside the gun was a magazine carrying 13 rounds. He was carrying two other full magazines for re-load inside his jacket. Syrnyk went into wounded animal mode, firing repeatedly and recklessly, the pop of each shot stinging his ears. His aim was wild, glass shattering in wild crescendos. He was not in control any longer, and was prepared to do anything necessary to regain it.

A 16-year-old boy was just walking into the mall when four gunshots rang out, followed by the sounds of women screaming. He dove for cover as double-pane glass exploded and shards began shooting through the air. The teen's thin, angular face was drawn tight, his eyes red-rimmed, his colour pale. "He's got a gun, he's got a gun," several people shouted from all directions, the panic evident in their voices. A couple of elderly women hit the frozen ground, ducking the barrage of bullets piercing the daytime air.

Kendall jumped behind a pillar, the sounds of the bandit's gunshots coming far too close. Kendall pulled out his own Smith and Wesson .38 calibre pistol, and felt he had no choice but to pull the trigger. Lives were at stake here, including his own.

Syrnyk knew he was on dangerous ground, having fallen directly in the open lot with nowhere to hide. He was prone, in no position to run, and the nine rounds he fired from his weapon only added to the confusion. But even with death staring him in the face, Syrnyk felt a rush of adrenaline, almost an eerie sense of calm.

Kendall fired five shots in all, but believed his gunfire was having no effect on the bandit. The return fire was coming faster than his own. With the situation getting more out-of-control by the second, he turned back towards the mall and began running. In the chaos, he dropped the money bag. Kendall saw the glass doors had been completely shot out, and saw the frightened masses of shoppers, several of whom were in the fetal position on the ground. Shell casings littered the snow-covered ground. Kendall went right through the blasted-out door, bashing his head on the exit bar in his haste to retreat to safer ground. He didn't feel the pain. Kendall feared the maniac was chasing after him, and didn't stop for even a second to check the blood streaming down from his head wound until he reached the Sears store. Only then did he turn around. He was relieved not to see the gunman. The entire incident had lasted 20 seconds. For all involved, it seemed like a lifetime.

The guard now out of sight, Syrnyk went straight for the money bag. As he ran, he felt a sting in his lower leg, around his ankle. Blood was trickling out through his pants. Syrnyk knew he'd been shot. He would fully assess the damage later, once he was on safe ground. But he knew this had not gone well, that his instincts were off. Clearly, the layoff had hurt him. Syrnyk, his visible agony from the injury masked to witnesses by the balaclava, brushed by several terrified people, including a teen boy and some seniors, as he ran towards the mall and eventually through the maze of shattered glass. As he hobbled through the mall, trying to position himself near his getaway car, Syrnyk was leaving a bloody trail behind. Nobody got in his way, customers parting like the Red Sea, some huddling against glass display cases and storefronts, others hiding behind banisters or staying down on the floor. Crimson streaks detailed his every move past three stores and into the MTS phone centre, where he fled out a rear entrance. Waiting outside in a nearby lane was a blue 1993 Dodge Shadow. Syrnyk jumped in, heading east, paying little attention to his wounded leg. He had made a clean getaway. But behind him, Syrnyk had left the smoking gun police had been hoping for – DNA.

● ● ● ● ● ●

Every available cruiser car in Winnipeg was ordered to Polo Park, and dozens of Winnipeg police officers rushed to the scene, sealing off all mall exits and containing the immediate area within minutes. Several officers searched the large parking lot and nearby streets. Checkpoints were set up on major city intersections and bridges, looking for the Dodge Shadow and a possible licence plate of BDA 833 that a witness had recorded. Police even searched the grounds of the Winnipeg International Airport, in case the bandit was looking to quickly get out of the city. A vague description was given to all airline staff. Back at the shopping mall, identification officers began combing the scene. Their main focus was the blood trail, which began just inside the mall doors and was continuous. Police quickly determined the blood was being cast off a moving object, likely the fleeing suspect. In the rear service hall, the stains were on the right side. Police believed the position and shapes of the blood meant the wound was to their suspect's lower right leg. The blood appeared to stop at the exit from the MTS office. Members of the Royal Canadian Mounted Police firearms lab were called to lend their expertise. Const. Darryl Barr arrived quickly from the nearby Portage Avenue headquarters and began working the extensive crime scene. The gunman had made a mighty mess.

Barr found six ejected nine-millimetre shell casings near the wall of the CIBC. An employee noticed a seventh a short time later. Three doors and an overhead window of the front entrance were shattered. A bullet lay beside an ashtray under the front door canopy, a place where nicotine-addicted shoppers had been standing when the shootout began. One bullet fragment was up against the wall of Sears, the biggest department store in the mall. Another was found beside the bike rack. There was a visible bullet impact on the side of a garbage can near the doors, while another fragment was found in the vestibule of the mall, just in front of a second set of doors. Barr noticed three markings in the packed snow, indicating bullets had ricocheted. Kendall's gun had also done plenty of damage. Barr found one of his shots had left a hole through the window of the Moxie's stairwell. The bullet ended up on the third step of the stairs. Another bullet and two impacts were found in a broken restaurant window. One of Kendall's shots had struck an office window of the CIBC, breaking the outer pane. Other bullet impacts were left in the base of two metal tree planters outside Moxie's, and a fragment was found on the ground outside the restaurant. The RCMP brought out a metal detector to sweep the area for anything they might have missed. All it confirmed was that police had done an extremely thorough job without a mechanical aid. Meanwhile, police were busy notifying all hospitals and walk-in clinics in Winnipeg, Saskatchewan and north-western Ontario to be on the lookout. The Canada-United States border crossing in Manitoba was also called. Everyone was on guard.

Terrified shoppers who witnessed the daytime mayhem had quite the stories to tell, some more eager and able than others to discuss what they had just seen. Numerous uniformed officers scattered throughout the mall, speaking to more than 40 people ranging from teenagers to seniors in their 70's. Their reports ranged from the droll to the dramatic.

"I heard this noise and saw a lady hitting the bricks by the entrance to the mall. There was about a four second pause and I saw another lady picking herself off the ground, and I thought someone's been shot. My wife was with me so I thought let's get out of here."

"Myself, my son and my daughter-in-law were going to Moxie's restaurant for lunch. We had just passed through the doors into the stairwell area, and a guy quickly brushed past me. I thought he was kind of rude, but I didn't pay too much attention to him. Shortly after that I heard multiple pops and heard glass breaking. My son and his wife at this point quickly shuffled me in behind the stairwell for protection, and we stayed there until things settled down."

"I heard this odd noise. I heard it about five times. I looked up. My friend said 'Holy Shit'."

"It was about noon and me and my friend went to Polo Park to get some lunch. As we were walking in the mall, I observed a security guard walking towards me by himself, carrying a bag. I mentioned to my friend I thought it was strange he was walking alone. Maybe 10 or 15 seconds went by when I heard three pops that sounded like firecrackers, coming from the same doorway we had just come in. I looked back and saw people screaming and running into the mall."

"I was just leaving the mall, with my son. I remember hearing a 'pop'. I ducked behind a planter.

The Yuletide Bandit

I kept my head down until my son told me to come with him back into the mall."

"I opened the door to the Moxie's stairwell and let my wife and mom in. Once I walked in I noticed the male running down the stairs. At first I thought he was just in hurry but then I saw him pull a pistol out of a bag."

"I had just put my bank card inside the instant teller machine at the CIBC. I was punching in my personal code when I heard repetitive popping sounds of glass breaking. I heard several people draw in their breath and then I realized something serious was taking place."

"I was at the Sears gift shop located across from the CIBC bank. I was bent down with my back to the CIBC looking at something on the rack when I heard a window smash behind me and people yelling and screaming. I immediately turned and saw people laying on the ground and the centre door window smashing out. I saw a woman lying on the ground just outside the doors by the pillar so I started to walk towards her. At that point someone yelled out he's got a gun or there's a gun and that's when I stopped walking towards the woman and crouched down in the mall area."

"My attention was drawn to a number of very loud bangs, that sounded like a cap gun, but very loud. I was looking towards the mall doors, and I saw something falling to the ground. My initial impression was that it was just ice falling off the building, and that was what I associate the noise to – breaking ice."

"I was in Carlton Cards fairly close to the front of the store when I heard a 'pop, pop' and glass shattering. I stepped forward and could see the glass coming down the security guard coming into the mall. He was running with his gun out."

"I was leaving the Polo Park Shopping Centre through the southeast exit, between Sears and the CIBC. I was looking south and was halfway through the courtyard when I heard shots that sounded like cap guns. I turned and saw a guy in a red jacket, shooting. He was shooting at the Brink's type guy over in the corner. The Brink's guy dove into the door to get away from the shooting."

"I was just walking into the mall. My sister and I were in between the outer and inner doors when I heard two shots. I turned around and saw two guys shooting at each other. I yelled to my sister, 'They have guns. They're shooting!' We ducked down and kept going through the inner doors and stopped in Carlton Cards."

Other witnesses described giving chase of the suspect, a risky and potentially fatal move which police frowned upon.

"He said that a guy with the bag…had just ran through the back door of MTS. We took off running through the MTS store and when we got to the back we could see the service door was open, loading into a service hallway. We ran straight down the hall to a closed door leading to the east parking lot of Polo Park. We never saw the guy in the hall, but as we got to the door I could hear a car speeding away."

"I was working at MTS and standing in the middle of the store. I saw a person run by me and he ran out the back door. I thought maybe he stole something from our store and I was going to go after him and yell at him. I could hear his big clumping boots echoing in the hallway. I was just about to yell at him when a co-worker yelled 'don't, he has a gun'."

Some witnesses described the culprit as 6'0, stocky, more than 200 pounds. Others figured he was only 5'6, lean, maybe 160 pounds. He was described as white. He was described as Filipino. He was described as East Indian. Some pegged him in his late teens or early 20s. Others suggested mid 40s. Perhaps the most bizarre suspect description came from a 20-year-old girl, who told police the bandit looked like "Leonardo DiCaprio – but with a wimpier looking build". The frailties of eyewitness examination were readily apparent on this day.

The most intriguing witness of all on this day was a dishevelled, 48-year-old man who approached police outside the mall a few hours after the mayhem. He identified himself as Thomas. The man told officers at the scene he'd been in the Pharmasave drug store, at the corner of Keewatin Street and Logan Avenue, around 1:30 p.m. The store was about a 15-minute drive from Polo Park. While waiting in line, Thomas claimed a woman in front of him was making a suspicious purchase. Rubber gloves, bandages, gauze, and other medical supplies one would use to treat a wound. Thomas described the woman as white, about 30 years old, with an average build and black hair. Police wasted no time in chasing down the tip, sending a unit to the store. They arrived at 4:30 p.m.. Officers spoke with the female clerk, who described the mysterious customer as a pretty white female, 25 to 35 years, with dirty blond shoulder lengthy curly hair. She was sure the hair was blond, not black as Thomas described. The clerk said the woman was very calm and relaxed, and bought $33.01 worth of medical supplies. She had paid in cash. "Are these the right supplies to close a bad cut?" the woman had asked the clerk before leaving. Police noticed there was a monitor on the counter and asked to see the videotape. "It's totally a fake. It's not hooked up to a VCR," said the clerk. There would be no video of the suspicious shopper.

A major development occurred late in the day, when police recovered 32 different surveillance tapes from the mall. Most showed little, or nothing. But one did stand out, capturing every dramatic detail of the wild shootout. As they viewed the tape, police were shocked they weren't investigating a mass murder.

The Polo Park security manager was able to delete unnecessary angles and get a clear image that showed the masked suspect, both before and after he was shot. It was a miracle nobody was killed. Police prepared to release copies of the tape to the media, hoping the dramatic images would break the case wide open. The Yuletide Bandit was about to go prime time.

Loomis guard Dale Lagimodiere is swarmed by media after being shot by the Yuletide Bandit at the Wal-Mart store at Kenaston and McGillivray Boulevards on Dec. 24, 1999.

A grainy image taken from a surveillance camera captures the beginning of an armoured car heist outside the Polo Park Shopping Centre on Dec. 12, 2000.

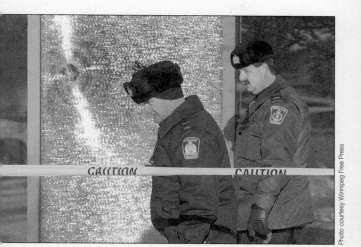

Winnipeg police officers walk by shattered pane of glass outside Polo Park Shopping Centre on Dec. 12, 2000.

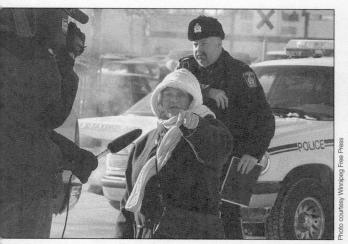

Elderly woman describes the daylight terror she witnessed while at Polo Park Shopping Centre on Dec. 12, 2000.

A Pharmasave employee shows the kind of medical supplies she sold to a mysterious woman believed to be helping a wounded Yuletide Bandit after he was shot on Dec. 12, 2000.

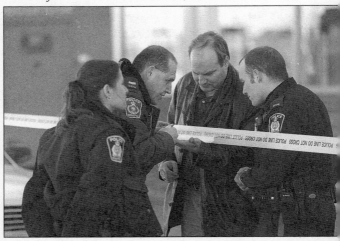

Police examine bullet fragments found at scene of Feb. 18, 2002 armoured car heist outside the Winnipeg Safeway store on Vermillion Road.

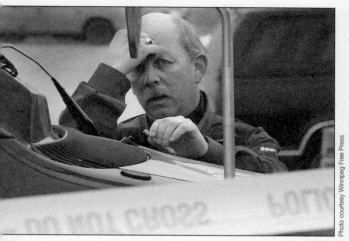

Securicor guard Rick Long catches his breath following dramatic robbery, shootout and gun chase outside McPhillips Street Safeway store on Apr. 7, 2002.

Police speak to shaken armoured car guard Serge Lechance about Apr. 7, 2002 robbery at Winnipeg Safeway store.

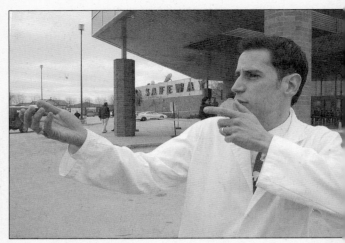

Employee at Winnipeg Safeway store describes wild shootout between the Yuletide Bandit and armoured car guards which occurred in the parking lot on Apr. 7, 2002.

The Yuletide Bandit's getaway car is examined by police following Apr. 7, 2002 robbery and car chase.

Heavily armed Winnipeg police officers take their positions outside downtown building where Yuletide Bandit and a hostage were holed up on May 1, 2002.

A frantic scene unfolds outside the Main Street building where two police officers were shot and wounded by the Yuletide Bandit on May 1, 2002.

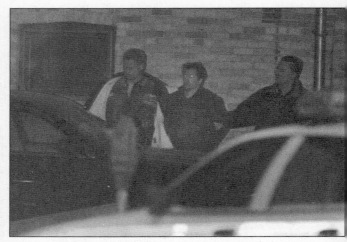

A dazed and confused Michael Syrnyk is taken away in handcuffs after police emergency response unit members stormed downtown building in the early morning hours of May 2, 2002.

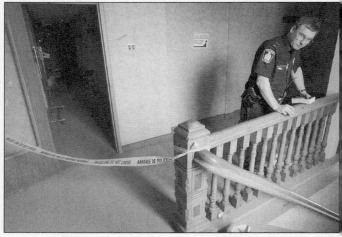

A police officer guards the scene directly outside the Club 205 massage parlour following a 13-hour standoff which ended May 2, 2002.

Mike Syrnyk Sr., the father of the Yuletide Bandit, answers his door to reporters following the arrest of his son.

The Yuletide Bandit, as a high school student (left), and following his arrest.

CHAPTER 13

December 13, 2000

On average, a car is stolen every hour in Winnipeg. The majority are recovered, usually within a few hours or days. Calls to police for abandoned and suspicious vehicles are about as common as calls to seedy Main Street bars for drunken, Friday night punch-ups. This particular call came into the police communications centre just after 9 a.m.. The 36-year-old man at the other end of the line was reporting an abandoned car sitting on the street outside his sister's home in the city's West End. It was a blue Dodge Shadow. "I had seen the description on the news last night which focused on the robbery and shooting that happened at the Polo Park Shopping Centre yesterday," the man told police. "I looked at the licence plate on the car and it is BDA 833. I remembered this was the licence plate released by the newscast last night that was associated with the stolen car at the robbery. I talked to my sister and she thinks that the car was parked here since yesterday afternoon." Two general patrol officers arrived on Ross Avenue moments later, an obvious sense of urgency in their work, and confirmed this was no routine dumped car case. They had the getaway car.

It looked like the robber must be hurt bad. The blood smeared throughout the car certainly told a painful story of the suspect's plight. Officers at the scene made a call to the identification unit, who asked for the car to be towed to the Public Safety Building for a more thorough examination. Police also took footwear impressions in the snow, which pointed in an easterly direction. Three distinct patterns were found, ranging in size from 25 centimetres to 31 centimetres. Given the potential for foot traffic in the suburban neighbourhood, they would likely be of little assistance.

At the Public Safety Building, police took swabs from 15 separate locations inside the car, including the gear shifter, glove box opener, passenger side sun visor, steering column, floor mat, door handles and turn signal. The driver's side carpet was completely red. Two tiny tissues, crumpled on the floor, showed of a pitiful attempt to treat the wounds. They likely had been saturated by blood within seconds and would have done little to stop the flow. Police wondered if the Yuletide Bandit wasn't on death's door.

• • • • • •

"Hello. Is there anybody in there? Just nod if you can hear me. Is there anyone home? Come on, now. I hear you're feeling down. Well I can ease your pain, Get you on your feet

again. Relax. I need some information first. Just the basic facts: Can you show me where it hurts? There is no pain, you are receding. A distant ship's smoke on the horizon.

You are only coming through in waves. Your lips move but I can't hear what you're sayin'. When I was a child I had a fever. My hands felt just like two balloons. Now I got that feeling once again. I can't explain, you would not understand. This is not how I am. I have become comfortably numb. Ok. Just a little pinprick. [ping] There'll be no more —aaaaaahhhhh! But you may feel a little sick. Can you stand up? I do believe it's working. Good. That'll keep you going for the show. Come on it's time to go. There is no pain, you are receding. A distant ship's smoke on the horizon. You are only coming through in waves. Your lips move but I can't hear what you're sayin'. When I was a child I caught a fleeting glimpse, out of the corner of my eye. I turned to look but it was gone. I cannot put my finger on it now. The child is grown, the dream is gone. I have become comfortably numb."

Michael Syrnyk was drifting in and out of consciousness as a Pink Floyd tape played in the background. The last 12 hours were somewhat blurry, an intense mix of pain and pleasure the like he'd never experienced before. There were moments Syrnyk felt like he was about to die as he watched the pulsating blood ooze from his wound. But he knew a doctor or hospital was out of the question. There were other moments he felt more alive then ever before. He would see a light and feel safe. On some cryptic level, Syrnyk was enjoying himself. The wound was gruesome, a small hole visible through his ankle near the Achilles tendon, indicating a point of entry and a point of exit. Clearly, it was going to leave a permanent scar. Syrnyk would have to be even more careful in the future.

He was literally a marked man.

The burning had subsided, having been numbed somewhat by peroxide, rubbing alcohol and medical bandages. At first, Syrnyk had wrapped duct tape around his leg, a band-aid solution if there ever was one that would have to do until he had his supplies. Syrnyk vowed to never tell anyone about how he was nursed back to health – but his good friend, Marlene Griffin, had come through when he needed her most.

Syrnyk flashed back to the shooting, his mind retracing every single detail. He saw a clear image of the man who shot him, his face remarkably calm during Syrnyk's ambush. *He was so cool*, thought Syrnyk. *Cooler than me anyways.* Syrnyk knew he would be laid up for a while, his ability to put pressure on his leg becoming more difficult by the hour. The money he'd grabbed from Polo Park would make the recovery easier. *This is going to lay me up for six months. But it's not going to stop me*, he vowed to himself.

• • • • • •

The Polo Park mayhem certainly had the media's attention now. Winnipeg radio and television stations had broken in with live coverage of the dramatic

The Yuletide Bandit

robbery. Both daily newspapers went all out in their morning editions, devoting several pages to stories and images that captured the magnitude of the brazen and shocking event. *"Panicked shoppers screamed and dove for cover while a robber and an armoured car guard exchanged gunfire at Polo Park Shopping Centre shortly after noon yesterday,"* the front-page *Winnipeg Free Press* story began. *"The robber, who police link to several Christmas-time armoured car heists in Winnipeg since 1998, left a trail of blood when he escaped with a bag of cash. Miraculously, nobody else in the bustling mall was hurt."* *"I'm still shaking,"* said an elderly woman who was in the bank at the time of the heist. I saw him through the window shooting and running and there was all this broken glass. He left blood all over the floor. It was very scary,"* the story continued. *"I saw this guy with a gun and I heard shots,"* said Henry, who was eating at the A&W restaurant on the second-floor of the mall and watched the incident play out below him through the window. *"It happened so fast I figured it was put on like a movie. But I know now, that was real."* *"We're anxious to get this guy off the streets as soon as possible,"* said police spokesman Const. Bob Johnson. *"We are using all available resources to catch him."* Police confirmed the bandit had been shot and wounded and pleaded with the public for help in ending his reign of terror. They released limited information about the woman seen buying medical supplies. *"A wounded outlaw was holed up somewhere in the city last night, possibly with help from a female accomplice,"* the *Free Press* story read. *"Police described the Yuletide Bandit as* *dangerous and probably unstable.*" There were a few paragraphs that were of particular concern to Syrnyk, who was carefully following the coverage of his crimes and actually felt proud of the attention he'd commanded. Police and medical officials described the high potential for infection if the wound was left untreated. Syrnyk, ever the worrier, began having moments of panic where he thought his foot might rot, perhaps even fall off.

● ● ● ● ● ●

Thomas had more information for police. One day after telling investigators about the woman buying medical supplies in Pharmasave, Thomas was back on the phone claiming he'd found more evidence. Thomas, it seemed, fancied himself as a modern-day Sherlock Holmes. He told police he'd spent the past few hours checking garbage bins in the back lane near his home, which was just down the block from the drug store. Thomas told a sergeant in the major crimes unit he had found bloody clothes in one of the dumpsters near a 7-Eleven.

Police raced to the scene, where Thomas produced his evidence – a spotless woman's sweatshirt and sweatpants. "They had absolutely no blood on them, and it was apparent at this time he doesn't have his full senses about him. These clothes had nothing to do with our case and his call was totally unfounded," police said in one of their reports. Fortunately, police had the Pharmasave clerk who confirmed Thomas's earlier version of events, otherwise that too would be in question. "It appears he is enjoying the attention he is receiving from police regarding this matter," police said of their "star" informant.

With the discovery of the stolen car, police began pounding the pavement in the immediate area of Polo Park, knocking on doors, desperate for any information. Officers planned to spend the next few days speaking with several hundred people. Many residents were obviously home but refused to answer. Police had no choice but to leave. Those who did open the door had little to offer. Police made special note of homes where young, blonde females were present, and were always checking for signs of injuries on any males who answered the door. A few things caught their eye. One man had his right knee in a bandage, claiming he'd just had surgery two days earlier. Police later confirmed his story. Another resident claimed he'd found blood behind his home. Police tested it and determined it wasn't blood. Another witness described a native male who purchased medical supplies from the Safeway store at Burrows Avenue and Keewatin Street the previous day, just hours after the hold-up. Another tipster claimed a fired Securicor employee matched the description of the woman seen buying medical supplies. Police printed a picture of the woman and showed it to the Pharmasave clerk, who was adamant she wasn't the customer. So many leads to chase, but all ultimately leading to the same dead end.

●●●●●●

The grainy video images of the Yuletide Bandit blasting away outside the crowded Polo Park quickly became the talk of the town, elevating the fears of a community already on edge. Television stations that had been provided the tape by police replayed the drama over and over in CNN-like fashion. It was the ultimate reality television. "We would really like to know who this guy is," Const. Bob Johnson told the media. "This guy is obviously a very dangerous individual."

Meanwhile, the robbery had armoured car guards even more on edge, and the political fallout was beginning as well. A guard with Brink's publicly accused armoured car companies of sacrificing safety to boost profits. Mike Blundell said armoured cars used to be staffed by three or four guards, but the number had been reduced to two in most cases. As was the case in the Polo Park incident, one of the two had to remain in the vehicle at all times. "That means you've got nobody to watch your back," Blundell told the media. "That's outrageous. We're just sitting ducks out there." His anger came as Brink's employees were out on strike, and Securicor guards were seeking mediation to resolve their own contract dispute. Guards earn on average between $10.75 and $12.46 an hour – "less than what a courier driver makes," Blundell said.

The public call for help was perhaps doing police more harm then good. Officers were being pulled from all districts to help chase down leads and

The Yuletide Bandit

theories, some which bordered on the absurd. On December 14, police got a tip that the bandit was holed up inside a north-end home. Five police units, including the canine team, met in the parking lot of the Merchants Hotel at the corner of Selkirk Avenue and Pritchard Street. They discussed a plan of action. The heavily-armed officers went to the nearby home and pounded on the door moments later. There was no immediate answer, so they kicked it in. Police found their supposed suspect inside his home, sitting on the couch. He was not injured, had an alibi, and was clearly the wrong man. "It would appear the anonymous caller had a vendetta against the individual as the information supplied was totally erroneous," police later reported. They left the scene, giving the angry homeowner a card with the number of the city claims office, who police suggested might be able to cover the damage done to his door.

Police responded to a report of blood on the street in the area, but ultimately traced it to a woman who had been stabbed in the hand by her husband and never reported the incident. On December 16, investigators went to Stony Mountain penitentiary to speak with an inmate who had called police, claiming to have information about the elusive bandit. The inmate claimed the suspect lived on Logan Avenue and was a "crazy guy" who had got his "old lady" to buy medical supplies for him. The information proved to be bogus, the product of yet another axe-to-grind.

Hours later, a tipster told police they might want to speak with a certain individual whom he believed had some information. Police tracked down the man, who was dumbfounded.

"He stated he knew nothing about the robbery at all, and that he had no idea why someone would say that he knew about the robbery," police said in their report. "Although, he said he would keep his ears open regarding it."

Then another tip came in, which seemed promising. The caller claimed a man named Clint, who had just been released from a Winnipeg drug and alcohol treatment centre, was responsible. He claimed Clint's girlfriend, Vera, was taking care of him. Police went to the treatment facility and were given a short list of four possible suspects all named Clinton. The men had been released in 1995, 1998, 1999 and October 2000. After much digging, none of them panned out.

On December 19, a caller claimed two brothers, whose names he provided, were assisting the Yuletide Bandit. Police tracked the men down the following day, and quickly discredited the caller's story. "A subsequent interview with the informant lead the informant to advise he had a personal grudge against the two men and was lying about his knowledge," police reported. However, the two falsely accused men gave police the name of another suspect they felt could be responsible. Police ran a record check on the man, and determined he fit the general suspect description.

The Yuletide Bandit

Their interest was heightened when they saw a conviction on his record – a 1992 robbery of a Loomis Armoured Car. There were several warrants out for the man's arrest, as he had gone AWOL from some court-ordered conditions in British Columbia. Alas, their hopes were dashed when police turned to science. The man's fingerprints were on file, and didn't match the ones police had taken from the Loomis robbery in 1999. Even worse, they had a sample of the man's hair, which didn't match the DNA they had from the spilled blood. Another brick wall.

Weeks later, another so-called informant crawled out of the woodwork and came to police with a potential lead. The man claimed he knew another man, who worked as a driver for an exotic dancer. The informant claimed the driver thought his girl was giving medical care to the bandit. Police chased down the driver, who didn't know what the hell they were talking about. It never seemed to end. And the result was police were still no closer to solving a case that seemed certain to end in tragedy.

CHAPTER 14

Michael Syrnyk's foot was healing at an incredible rate, considering it hadn't been looked at by anyone with a medical degree. Just some tender loving care at home, courtesy of Marlene Griffin. Syrnyk was permanently off the couch by February, less than two months after the man whose face he would never forget hit one of the few spots on his body that wasn't covered by armour. Syrnyk had thought a lot about the guard since the shooting, and actually felt some respect and admiration for what the man had done. It had been a great shot, and Syrnyk felt he actually deserved it. He was getting sloppy, careless and reckless, and the shooting was the most dramatic wake-up call to date. There was no anger, only an ongoing sense of self-frustration that was nothing new to Syrnyk. Although he had enjoyed success in the past, Syrnyk instead focused on the colossal failures that seemed to be mounting.

The time spent recovering from the injury had given Syrnyk more time to sort through the messy situation with Marlene and the children.

Conversations were growing deeper and more personal with each passing day, and Marlene clearly was in love. She had said as much. Syrnyk also told Marlene he loved her, and he did. More than any woman he'd ever been involved with. But Syrnyk didn't feel like his love was worth much, if anything. He didn't think he had much to give, and wondered why anyone would want to receive it. Syrnyk was providing for the family, in more ways than one. Money was no object, and Syrnyk was beginning to feel a sense of responsibility to support Marlene and the kids. But it was the emotional commitment that he was having more difficulty with. Just when they'd seem to grow closer, Syrnyk would pull back, unable to face the prospect of taking the next step. He really hit the wall the day Marlene brought up the prospect of having a child together.

Marlene had her tubes tied following the birth of her last child, figuring three was enough for one woman to handle, especially someone whose partner had walked out on her. But meeting Syrnyk had changed her feelings. There was a certain attraction to the obvious "bad boy" image he projected, but Marlene much preferred the softer side of Syrnyk she was seeing on a regular basis, especially when he was with her children. Syrnyk was so nurturing and caring, and Marlene felt the next step was to give Syrnyk a child of his own. It seemed crazy, but Marlene felt they could make it work. She hoped the dramatic event could trigger a lifestyle change for the better, pulling

Syrnyk into a family situation he wouldn't want to leave. So, Marlene began making plans to return to the hospital to have her tubes untied.

Syrnyk didn't feel like he was even close to being ready for parenthood. In fact, there were times spent with Marlene's children where he simply felt like the fourth child, more comfortable in their simple world than his own. He couldn't discipline the children, tell them it was time to go to bed, or really do anything he worried might cause himself to fall out of their favour. Syrnyk wondered how such a monster, such a shallow, self-obsessed little bastard like himself could parent a child? Yet Marlene seemed so sure, so confident, and Syrnyk wanted so much to please her. In the days ahead, Syrnyk began to fantasize about a crazy double-life where he could continue to be a ruthless, take-no-prisoners rebel, but also a caring father and partner. Syrnyk eventually told Marlene what she wanted to hear – he wouldn't be adverse to trying to make a baby with her.

● ● ● ● ● ●

Syrnyk stopped briefly outside the tattoo parlour, admiring the designs in the window, before walking inside. He knew exactly what he wanted. Two triangles, symbolizing trinity, on each wrist. One would be blue. The other would be red. Syrnyk had never thought much of tattoos, believing them to be a filthy, grimy practice that violated everything he believed in about keeping your body clean. Those beliefs seemed light years away now. The artist went to work, taking the needle directly to Syrnyk's gaunt wrists, right above where several veins were protruding. Syrnyk hardly felt a thing, thanks largely to the ecstasy he had taken prior to arriving. In fact, the little pain he was experiencing was actually enjoyable. Blue meant good. Red meant evil. Blue meant life. Red meant death. Blue meant love. Red meant fear. Blue meant consistency. Red meant change. To Syrnyk, the tattoos were much more than just designs on his skin. They were the story of his life.

• • • • • •

The thought of a happy life together with Marlene and the kids was too much for Syrnyk on this night. High on drugs and down on life, Syrnyk decided he was a criminal, not a family man. It was time to get his priorities straight again. He'd gone soft these past few months, and knew it had to end. Syrnyk wasn't ready to try another armoured car, his confidence still shaken by the Christmas chaos at Polo Park. He couldn't face the prospect of staring down another desperate, armed guard – at least not yet. Syrnyk decided to do something simpler, more basic, to restore his fragile ego.

March 21, 2001

It was just before 9 p.m. and only a couple customers were left inside the People's Jewellers store as it prepared to say good-night to another business day. Syrnyk was lurking outside, a shotgun strapped to his arm which was covered by a jacket. A sledgehammer was also hidden underneath. He was stone cold sober, and as nervous as ever. Syrnyk was hoping to wait until all the customers had left, but risked having the doors locked if he waited too long. So he pounced, running into the store directly towards the front counter. He pulled the sledgehammer out, taking a mighty swing at the glass display case housing a collection of necklaces and bracelets. The glass shattered as frightened staff and customers backed away. Syrnyk was holding the shotgun in the other hand, pointing it directly towards a middle-aged man who was standing nearby and had a cellular phone to his ear. Syrnyk assumed the customer was calling police.

He stared down the man, but had no intention of shooting him. Syrnyk couldn't justify taking a shot at someone who wasn't armed. He focused back on the display case, using his free hand to reach inside and grab a few pieces of jewellery. Syrnyk winced in pain as a shard of broken glass sliced through his hand. Blood began pouring out quickly, pooling in both the display case and on the floor beneath Syrnyk. He quickly retreated out the store, carrying a handful of gold necklaces but once again leaving something far more valuable behind. His DNA.

Winnipeg police were speechless. Their sophisticated Yuletide Bandit was now a sloppy, smash-and-grab artist? Blood samples taken from the scene of the jewellery store robbery stunned investigators when they were found to be a perfect match to the blood found inside the stolen car recovered after the Polo Park shootout. It was a completely unexpected development; one that was now forcing police to re-evaluate their theories on what exactly was going on here. Major crime detectives thought the bandit was likely a sophisticated criminal who was clearly putting a lot of planning into his crimes. He was probably a loner, and likely a first-timer given that no matches to his DNA were found in their computer system. But now police were wondering if the man wasn't just some typical crackhead looking for his next fix. How else to explain the motivation behind such a poorly executed and seemingly desperate crime? One thing was for certain – the Yuletide Bandit was back on his feet. And despite his apparent injury, he was still able to keep one step ahead of an entire police service desperate to bring him to justice.

• • • • • •

Syrnyk's hand was coming along nicely, but his mind was not. The physical wound had run deep, the emotional ones even deeper. Syrnyk was once again sinking back into a terrible depression, a feeling that his world was once again collapsing. Even the warm embrace of Marlene, or the innocent laughter of the children, couldn't get Syrnyk out of his personal hell. In fact, they only made things worse. At the top of his worries was a feeling police were soon going to catch him. Syrnyk knew his mistakes were piling up, as was the evidence against him.

So many ideas were running through his head. He could find some dupe, some lowlife on the street who was willing to give him blood in exchange for some money. Then Syrnyk could plant the blood in a car he would deliberately leave behind, and hope it throws police off track. Perhaps he could buy some cocaine, a drug he knew was easy to find in Winnipeg but still had never tried, and plant it in the car as well. Let the police think they were dealing with a drug addict. Syrnyk was certain of one thing – his relationship with Marlene was taking away the edge that had made him so successful. He was losing his instincts, and if he wasn't careful he would soon be losing his freedom, or maybe his life.

● ● ● ● ● ●

"I'm pregnant." Tears flowed down Syrnyk's face as Marlene told him the news. They were not tears of joy. Syrnyk had expressed himself the same way only weeks earlier, the night he now realized they had conceived. He had done it because Marlene wanted it, because she had done so much for him and he felt like he couldn't let her down. Now Marlene was beaming with happiness, which only sunk Syrnyk into deeper despair. He took Marlene in his arms, held her tightly, and then said good-bye. And walked straight out the front door and into the dark night, not knowing if he was ever coming back.

CHAPTER 15

September 11, 2001

Gruesome images of two hijacked airplanes striking the Twin Towers in New York City were playing continuously as news anchors tried to make sense of the enormous tragedy which was unfolding on live television. America was under attack. Michael Syrnyk sat alone in his living room, his eyes fixed on the movie-like reality which was unfolding before him. *The world is coming to an end*, he thought. In many ways, he wished it would.

Syrnyk spent the entire day staring at the television screen, watching as the Twin Towers fell to the ground, reports rolled in about more hijacked planes crashing, and Americans declared war on an unknown enemy which had just slaughtered thousands of innocent people. At times, Syrnyk pictured himself in the cockpit of the doomed airliners.

The past few weeks had been a terrible stretch for Syrnyk, beginning when he walked out on Marlene Griffin at the news they were going to have a child together. She miscarried weeks later. Marlene was upset, but not angry. She was more concerned about the fragile state of the man she loved. Syrnyk blamed himself, figuring the enormous stress he'd caused Marlene by walking out had led to the loss of their child. He would never forgive himself, proving once again he was a coward worthy of nothing.

• • • • • •

September 19, 2001

Virginia Syrnyk was dead. A nearly two-year fight for survival had mercifully ended, the disease simply proving too much to overcome. Cancer had claimed another innocent victim, sent another family into mourning. The entire Syrnyk clan had gathered at her hospital bedside in the late evening, knowing death was near and saying tearful good-byes. The phone call to Syrnyk, confirming his mother's passing, had come in the early morning hours.

The lone bright spot for the Syrnyk family had been a reunion, of sorts, between Virginia and Mike Sr.. Although living apart, the estranged couple seemed to become friends – for the first time – as Virginia slowly lost her battle. Mike Sr. was paying regular visits, both to the home and hospital, and he and Virginia would share long chats. Little was said about their terrible history, the couple instead wanting to focus on the present. Unfortunately, there was no future for Virginia. Mike Sr. hadn't complained the day he watched his car get towed from a no-parking zone as he sat in Virginia's hospital room. The old Mike Sr. probably would have gone off on a tirade. Instead, he cracked a smile as his wife cackled hysterically from her bed. He would bring Virginia food, buy her medicine and run errands. There were nights he even fell asleep in her hospital room. Talk often turned to their two children, and both Virginia and Mike Sr. were deeply worried about Michael, who had become an enigma to them.

Mourning didn't begin to describe Syrnyk's reaction to his mother's passing. It was pure manic. There had been too much loss, too much pain, for him to bear. He'd watched his mother waste away before his eyes and been helpless to stop her suffering. Life had never seemed so cruel.

• • • • • •

Marvin Simmons throws open his doors on a daily basis to the most down-and-out in society, forgotten souls who need reminding and reassuring that someone does indeed care about them. A friendly, easy-going senior with a gift for both speaking and listening, the reverend takes immense pride in the work he does. There are many faces he sees once, then never again. Simmons often lies awake wondering what has become of them. Worrying for them. Praying for them. There are many others who keep coming back, clearly moved by the experience inside the Wide World Of Faith Church, located on Alexander Avenue in one of Winnipeg's most downtrodden neighbourhoods. Simmons fights hard to keep the converted believers in his pews, a place where he assures them they are safe and loved. There are many followers who make a lasting impact on Simmons, names and faces he will never forget. Then there are the Michael Syrnyk's of the world.

Syrnyk walked into the church, not really sure how long he was going to stay or what exactly he was here to do. His mother's death was weighing heavily on his mind, as were thoughts of the harm he'd caused others and how ashamed his mother would be of him. A friendly face greeted him upon his arrival, the man quickly introducing himself as Rev. Simmons. Syrnyk had difficulty making eye contact, staring mostly at the ground. He was feeling extremely uncomfortable, instantly regretting the decision to walk in. The reverend sensed something was wrong with the scruffy-faced stranger and invited him to sit down and chat. Syrnyk reluctantly took a seat. For the first few minutes, Syrnyk said very little, simply nodding his head as the reverend explained the workings of the church and its function in the community. Syrnyk told the man he was thinking about joining a congregation, and might be interested in attending some services. The reverend said he was welcome. As the conversation continued on, Syrnyk was fighting the increasing urge to say more. There was so much bottled up inside, so much he wanted to tell. "Do you know that Syrnyk means 'He who is like God'?" asked Syrnyk. The reverend nodded.

The reverend seemed like a trusting soul, someone who wouldn't judge him the way he believed most of society had. Right now, he was all Syrnyk had. So Syrnyk began speaking. "I've betrayed a woman I love," he offered quietly. It hurt him just to say the words. He explained the miscarriage, which he believed was caused by walking out on Marlene. He told the reverend of the enormous guilt he was carrying. "It's so hard for me to believe someone so wonderful wanted to be with me," said Syrnyk. He mentioned that he had betrayed some innocent people as well, but offered up nothing more. So much of him wanted to tell the whole story, just finally get it out into the open. Not now. Not yet. The reverend simply listened, offered a few kind words of support, and invited Syrnyk to return. Syrnyk agreed that he would. He left the church, his mind feeling somewhat less cluttered but still wrestling with his next move.

• • • • • •

The man seated directly across from Syrnyk had a puzzled look on his face as he tried to process the bizarre request. "You want me to do what?" the man asked, obviously questioning whether his ears had just deceived him. They hadn't, but Syrnyk repeated his question anyways.

"I want you to put me under, and read me *Paradise Lost* so I remember it." Syrnyk said. He was oblivious to the fact that what he was asking this hypnotherapist was not only ridiculous but also pretty much impossible. *Paradise Lost* was enormous, to the point Syrnyk would have to be put under for days. "Can you do it?" an impatient Syrnyk asked. The trips to church had Syrnyk thinking a lot about his favourite book again, the ongoing battle between God and Lucifer, good and evil. The story was intense, and Syrnyk was relating more than ever to it – at least the parts he could remember. He believed Adam and Eve might have contemplated suicide at one point, likely experiencing the same tortured feelings he was having now. But Syrnyk's biggest obstacle was his own failing memory, which seemed to be getting worse as he delved deeper into drugs. His emotional instability was also a factor. Syrnyk wanted the hypnotherapist to increase his memory and literally plant the book in his head so he would never forget it. The puzzled man explained Syrnyk's request was both unusual and extremely difficult, and suggested an alternative. He would put Syrnyk under, but instead of reading the book line by line, would instead focus on mind control and knowledge retention, which he explained would give Syrnyk the tools to expand his memory base. Syrnyk sat back in the chair, closed his eyes and began to listen to the man speak.

● ● ● ● ● ●

The snow was falling gently to the ground, giant fluffy flakes blowing in a gentle, cold breeze. Syrnyk walked slowly through the cemetery, passing dozens of white-topped gravestones as he headed towards the crucifix. As he neared the statue, Syrnyk fell to his knees. He looked straight up into the grey sky, clasped his hands together, and begged God to forgive him. Tears rolled down his red cheeks, the salty remnants collecting on his lips. He took his right hand and carefully reached into his jacket pocket. Syrnyk was holding a handgun. He'd already loaded a bullet into the chamber. Syrnyk cocked the weapon as he raised it to his right temple. He felt the cold steel against the side of his head. Then he squeezed the trigger.

Syrnyk jolted back to reality, unable to complete the horrible mental picture he had conjured up. Even in his darkest thoughts, Syrnyk was still a coward. On the table beside him was an open bottle of morphine. Just as his mother had done, Syrnyk was now using the powerful drug to block out his pain. Only his was emotional, not physical.

Syrnyk hit drugs hard following his mother's death, unable to cope with so much loss and his own personal failures. His new favourite was his mother's leftover morphine, which seemed to intensify his emotions and take Syrnyk right to the brink of mental anarchy. As an eventful 2001 was drawing to a close, Syrnyk found himself contemplating an unexpected ally, one he thought he would never call upon. Cocaine.

● ● ● ● ● ●

A drive from St. James to downtown Winnipeg will usually take about 10 minutes, depending on how many green lights you catch and how busy traffic on Portage Avenue is. For Syrnyk, the trip could take an entire day. As winter's icy grip began taking hold of Winnipeg for another long, dreary season, Syrnyk began spending more and more time outdoors, always alone and on foot. He would get up in the morning, get dressed and leave his home, usually with no real destination in sight. He would usually pop a morphine pill or two before he left. Syrnyk would walk briskly, taking little time to stop and take in the scenery.

One afternoon, Syrnyk was headed to see Reverend Simmons at his inner-city church when he stopped walking at the sight of a large structure just up the road. It was the Public Safety Building, the headquarters for the Winnipeg Police Service. A sense of guilt quickly washed over Syrnyk. But so too did a feeling of opportunity. Here was his chance to make things right, to end the suffering and begin rebuilding whatever was left of his life. All he had to do was walk through the doors.

Syrnyk began moving again, though at a much slower pace. He neared the front of the building, where some uniformed front-desk officers were smoking cigarettes. Several marked police cars were nearby, including some pulling out of the basement garage and on to the street. Syrnyk looked around, carefully studying everything around him. Then he turned around and walked away.

· · · · · ·

Christmas 2001 came to pass without any activity from the Yuletide Bandit. Everyone – from police to

The Yuletide Bandit

armoured car guards to store merchants – had been on guard, expecting another violent attack. Police had stepped up patrols once again in areas of concern, namely shopping malls and major retail outlets where large volumes of money were coming and going daily. The general public had been warned to be wary of any suspicious activity, and to immediately report anything they might see. Plenty of calls came in to police, but nothing of any substance. Paranoia combined with past history clearly had people on edge. Police were quite puzzled by the lack of activity, wondering what had become of their elusive bandit. It wasn't like him to stay quiet for so long. It was as if he'd fallen off the face of the earth.

CHAPTER 16

February 18, 2002

Curtis Hourd took a final drag on his cigarette, anxious to escape the cold and get back inside his busy south Winnipeg Safeway store. It was noon, and business was about to pick up as customers on their lunch breaks began running errands they hadn't got to during the just completed weekend. Hourd – the store manager – dropped his cigarette butt in the ashtray just outside the main doors before walking in, greeting several customers with a smile. Most returned the friendly gesture. This stone-faced Securicor guard did not. The man, whom Hourd had never seen before, appeared to be very young and most serious. Hourd had passed the guard moments earlier on his way outside for a smoke, even saying "Hello" when they were within a few feet of each other. But the man had said nothing in return, staring straight ahead as he carried an empty bag inside to pick up the cash deposits. Now the guard was leaving the store, the bag full. His expression hadn't changed. Hourd was slightly taken aback, as the guards who frequent his store are usually quite friendly, greeting Safeway staff with a wave or a smile, even stopping to chat briefly. But not today.

The cocaine had kicked in. Michael Syrnyk was twitching with anxiety and anticipation as he crouched down in the back of the mini-van he'd stolen days earlier. A dark sheet was covering his body. Syrnyk had a perfect view of the scene outside, and was just waiting for the time to strike. He was ready to make his comeback.

The Securicor truck had pulled into the parking lot right on schedule, and Syrnyk watched the lone guard walk inside Safeway while his partner waited behind the wheel.

Syrnyk knew he would only be a couple minutes, having timed the Safeway run from start to finish during several "scouting" missions over the past few days. He was more excited about this robbery than perhaps any of the others, the drugs giving him a newfound feeling of invincibility and cockiness. He was ready for anything. Syrnyk braced himself as he watched the guard come through the main doors and head back into the parking lot.

Their workday was only five hours old, but already Mark Swaffer and Ralph Hordyski were on their 20th pickup. Robin's Donuts, Payroll Loans, the Dakota Hotel, McDermot Lumber, the Disney Store, Sears, Wal-Mart, Shopper's Drug Mart, 7-Eleven, Home Depot, Branigans Restaurant, Zellers, a few liquor stores and a social hall were under their belts. Tens of thousands of dollars was tucked away in the back of their marked truck. Swaffer, 20, had only started working with Securicor 15 months earlier but felt like it had been much longer. Going to work filled with fear will do that to a man. And Swaffer, who was only on part-time, certainly had his share of worries given the recent work environment for armoured car guards. His $15.85 per hour wage hardly compensated for the constant paranoia that was plaguing him and most of his co-workers, ever since the Yuletide Bandit arrived on scene. The fact a Christmas had passed without any problems did little to ease the concerns of guards, who would only rest easy knowing the man had been caught. Or was dead.

Ralph Hordyski, 56, wasn't as high-strung, thanks largely to decades of job experience and a strong feeling that he could take care of himself should the situation arise. He'd dealt with his share of bad-asses before retiring several years earlier as a guard at Stony Mountain penitentiary. Although he had only started with Securicor nine months ago, Hordyski wasn't going to be intimidated. He also felt more comfortable around a gun then most of his co-workers, based on 16 years of work as a firearms instructor and his current role as a part-time gunsmith. Hordyski wouldn't hesitate for a heartbeat to use his weapon.

He was driving the truck today, with Swaffer going into the stores to make the drop-offs and pickups. The duo had arrived at the Vermillion Road

Safeway around 11:55 a.m., and Swaffer went into the back of the truck to prepare numerous rolls of coins he was leaving at the store. Swaffer then went inside while Hordyski stayed behind in the truck, surveying the scene to ensure a safe exit route for his partner. Two minutes passed. Hordyski saw nothing out of the ordinary, but took another detailed look when Swaffer appeared at the door, bag in hand, preparing to walk outside. A sudden movement in the rear-view mirror caught Hordyski's eye. He turned to see a man, dressed in dark clothing, running quickly towards his partner.

Syrnyk was counting on the element of surprise – but the expression on the young guard's face suggested a very different emotion. Anger. The shotgun at his side, Syrnyk was in a full running stride as he neared his prey. But he put the brakes on when the man reached to his side and pulled out a handgun. The guard wasn't going down without a fight.

It had boiled down to a simple question – my life or his? For Swaffer, the answer was easy. He dropped the money bag, freeing up both his hands to hold his .38-calibre weapon as he saw the masked gunman running towards him. Swaffer squeezed the trigger two times, taking aim at the dark silhouette that was coming for him. He was trying to quickly move backwards, to find cover at the front of the grocery store. Swaffer fired twice more as he back-pedalled.

A bullet kissed Syrnyk's cheek, grazing his cloth-covered mug ever so slightly. An inch or two to the side and he would have been dead. But Syrnyk was still breathing, and he had plenty of fight in him today. He aimed his shotgun at the fleeing guard and began blasting away. He was oblivious to the gunshots still coming in his direction.

"Duck, duck behind here. Get down!" The frightened female Safeway cashier screamed at her customers in line as the sound of gunshots rang out from the front of the store. Several people, including some senior citizens, took her advice and hit the floor. It appeared a wild gunfight was going down outside. Hourd, the Safeway store manager, was about to go up the stairs to his office when at least nine loud popping sounds rang out. The sound was muffled, but Hourd was sure it was gunfire. There had been too many for it to be anything else, such as a car backfiring. Hourd turned around, walked back onto the floor of the store and saw one of his regular customers talking quickly on her cellular phone. "It's 911," she said. "The police are coming." Hourd continued walking, and then saw the Securicor guard he'd passed moments earlier standing just inside the doors of his store, holding a handgun and pointing it out towards the parking lot.

Brian Goodman, 22, was driving his grandmother's silver Dodge Shadow through the Safeway parking towards the Canadian Tire Store. The elderly woman was sitting in the passenger seat. They both jolted at the sound of several loud bangs. At first Goodman thought a car had backfired. Then he turned around to see the rear windshield had been completely shattered by a stray bullet.

Syrnyk was still firing at the guard, who moved quickly through the doors of the Safeway store and back inside. He was out of range. Syrnyk took a quick look around the parking lot, where several customers and cars had come to a frightened standstill. He saw the bulky Securicor bag lying on the ground, several metres ahead near the entrance. He desperately wanted to grab it, but knew the risk was great.

Swaffer's heart was nearly jumping out of his chest as he stood inside the front doors, keeping a watchful eye on the masked man with the shotgun through the glass. He was emptying the remaining bullets from his gun and reloading with a speed loader, which he carried on his gun belt. Swaffer wasn't going to be outgunned. The weapons upgrade became moot, however, as Swaffer saw the bandit rush to the bag on the ground, scoop it up and then retreat to a parking space near the Securicor truck. The gunman jumped in through the rear hatch of a dirty white mini-van, which had been down but not latched. He still had the shotgun in his hand. The van sped away, heading west through the parking lot and then out of sight. Swaffer couldn't see the licence plate number. He stood at the store windows, staring blankly into the parking lot.

Swaffer's two-way radio began to crackle. "Are you okay?" It was Hordyski, still sitting inside the Securicor truck as per company policy. "Yeah, I'm fine. I'm not hit," Swaffer replied, although he hadn't checked himself over to make sure that was even true. In fact, Swaffer just noticed one of his toes was stinging a bit. He wasn't sure if he'd stubbed it or if it was grazed by the return gunfire, but would worry about it later.

A handful of Safeway employees who'd heard the gunfire approached the visibly shaken guard asking him if he was hurt. "Holy shit. I never thought this would happen to me," Swaffer told the store manager. "Has somebody called 911?" one of the other Safeway workers asked. They had. Swaffer could only hear murmuring, his eyes and thoughts still fixated on the parking lot. He began to walk outside, taking slow, methodical steps. The ground was littered with spent shotgun shells. Swaffer noticed a black piece of cloth that he thought might have fallen off the bandit. A stranger walked up to Swaffer, holding four spent shells in his hand and giving them to the guard. Another customer pointed out what appeared to be an unspent shell, near the main door. Swaffer put the items in his pocket. Another man approached, this time an employee of the Canadian Tire store that shared the same parking lot. He was holding a small piece of lead, likely a shotgun pellet, and told Swaffer it had grazed his leg. The man had literally dodged a bullet.

Winnipeg police scattered in all directions, many taking the immediate scene while others dispatched to roadside checkpoints in the area. Witnesses believed the getaway vehicle could be a Dodge Caravan, but without a licence plate it was going to be a difficult search. A 15-year-old exchange student from France certainly got an education in real-life crime, describing the events he'd just witnessed to police while waiting for his host mother to finish shopping inside the store. "The van was dirty white, but I don't know what kind of van, I didn't really see it that well because I was running back into the store," the terrified teen told officers.

Another young man approached police, saying he'd witnessed the incident. He had parked his car to grab some groceries when the shootout began. Some of the shots were landing near his vehicle. The witness thought the culprit was about 5'7 with a skinny build, but admitted his recollection might be a little off. The man told police he suffers from epilepsy, and has difficulty remembering things following a stressful event.

An elderly woman told officers she was in the Safeway store when the hold-up happened, and had noticed a suspicious looking teenager standing nervously near the customer service desk just moments earlier. Police thanked the woman for her help, but knew they weren't dealing with some acne-faced teen. They were dealing with a professional. Police pretty much disregarded another witness description that painted the bandit as a chubby, balding man in his late 40s or early 50s. Just like the Polo Park robbery had proven, eyewitness evidence was proving to be fragile at best.

The Yuletide Bandit

Another woman waved down police in the parking lot and provided officers with their most interesting lead of the day. She had been just west of the Safeway when the robbery occurred, and watched the bandit run towards the front of the store to confront the guards. The woman said one thing stood out in her mind about the man. A noticeable limp.

Another man told police he thought the suspect was both screaming and laughing as he ran off to his waiting getaway car. He also described the suspect as having a limp. Although there really wasn't any doubt, the witnesses' description of an injured leg virtually assured police the Yuletide Bandit was involved.

Police began a canvas of neighbouring businesses, asking everyone if they had operating surveillance cameras that might have captured some of the incident on tape. Two businesses had exterior closed-circuit television cameras that simply played images back in real-time but did not record. Seven other merchants either didn't have cameras at all, or only had interior cameras. Three businesses did have working exterior cameras that recorded images. Unfortunately, the shootout had been out of their camera's reach.

Police also began taking detailed statements from the two Securicor guards. Hordyski described the bandit as 5'7 to 5'9, with a medium build. Swaffer figured he was taller, but definitely less than 6'2. He believed he was white, and young. "Why did you fire your weapon?" an officer asked Swaffer. Swaffer took offence to the question but didn't have to think twice about an answer. "I saw someone running at me with a shotgun pointed at me. I felt my life was in immediate danger," he said. Hordyski backed his partner up, saying he thought the robber would have killed Swaffer. "When Mark was back-peddling after he saw this perpetrator he quickly moved to the side. I think that's what caused the perpetrator to miss. I don't think he expected Mark to miss like that. It probably saved his life," said Hordyski.

Swaffer told police he wasn't very familiar with his weapon, because Securicor only gives guns to full-time employees. Part-timers like him simply pick one up from the company before the start of each shift. He also wasn't wearing a bullet-proof vest. In fact, he didn't own one, and Securicor didn't supply their guards with one. Police told him he was lucky to have escaped injury, or even death. Swaffer nodded his head. Police wanted his gun, ammunition and work boots for forensic examination. They also wanted him to come to the Public Safety Building to give a more detailed statement. Swaffer agreed, and asked the officers when he could use a telephone. He wanted to call his mother.

● ● ● ● ● ●

Winnipeg police Const. James Kitchen heard the getaway car description over his police radio and was keeping his eyes peeled for any signs of a white Dodge Caravan. It was 3:44 p.m., approaching four hours since the robbery had occurred. Kitchen was driving west on Vermillion Road, near the Safeway store, when some skid marks on the pavement got his attention near the intersection of Lakewood Boulevard. The markings appeared to cross Lakewood westbound on to Weatherstone Road. Kitchen followed the trail, proceeding west on Weatherstone, and quickly hit the jackpot. Parked on the north side of the road was a white Dodge Caravan.

Kitchen radioed in to the communications centre and drew his weapon. The van appeared to be empty, but he wasn't taking any chances. He moved to the front of van, placing his hand on the hood. It was warm to the touch. The engine hadn't been shut off for very long. Kitchen went to the side, finding all the doors were unlocked. He could see the ignition switch on the left hand side of the steering column had been punched and removed. He opened the sliding side door, taking a hard look to ensure nobody was hiding inside. Kitchen got a brief scare by a lumpy bag of hockey equipment sitting in the back. Several pieces of equipment were also scattered throughout the van. He continued on, scanning the front part of the van where he noticed a blue toque lying on the floor. Kitchen was about to return to his own vehicle to check for further information about the stolen vehicle when he spotted a small piece of white paper sitting on the driver's side seat. He took a closer look, and read the robber's defiant challenge to police: "WHY DON'T YOU BLOW ME AND TAKE ANOTHER SAMPLE."

CHAPTER 17

Winnipeg's two daily newspapers – the broadsheet *Free Press* and tabloid *Sun* – were spread out on the coffee table. A small pile of powdered cocaine sat nearby. Michael Syrnyk sat slumped on the couch, dishevelled and somewhat disoriented after going for what seemed like days without sleep. He was coming down off a series of highs, all energy now drained from his body. Syrnyk's swollen, red eyes gazed at the front page of the papers, which told dramatic stories of his latest conquest. Numerous witnesses described what they had witnessed. *"I was in the Safeway, paying for my groceries, when all of a sudden I hear bang, bang, bang, four or five shots."* said one man. *"I saw the guy running with the rifle in the air past the window. Someone said 'Get down!' and we all got down. A lot of people were shaken up,"* said a Safeway employee, adding the store had never been robbed during her 18 years of employment. A young man and his grandmother told of the horror of having their back window shot out as they drove through the parking lot. *"I couldn't believe it. I'm just glad my grandmother and I weren't hurt,"* the man said. *"We're alive, thank goodness. I was really scared,"* added his shaken granny. Syrnyk felt little empathy towards his victims, the cocaine masking any real emotions. He snorted another line.

Syrnyk did twig to news police had found his car. There was no mention of the note. Syrnyk only thought of leaving the taunting scrap of paper during his frantic run for freedom. Maybe it was the adrenaline – most likely it was the cocaine – but he couldn't resist the urge to let police know who was in control. He wished he could have seen the expression on the officers' faces when they found it, knowing they must be burning inside at their utter failure to catch him. Police admitted in the newspaper stories they had the bandit's DNA but had been unable to get a match. Investigators were also quoted saying they thought the bandit might have been struck by one of the guard's bullets, as he was seen limping away from the scene. If only they knew how close.

The stories also gave Syrnyk some insight, for the first time, into what police actually knew about him. Until now, he'd never made a point of really monitoring what the media was saying about his crimes, as sober second thoughts about many of the robberies left him wanting to escape the reality of what he'd done. But no more. Syrnyk was now anxious to see how he was being portrayed in a city that surely must be in fear and awe of what he's accomplished. He scanned through the various reports. *"Const. Bob Johnson said the robbery is similar to past hold-ups in Winnipeg since 1998, particularly the hold-ups at Polo*

The Yuletide Bandit

Park and outside a Wal-Mart store Dec. 24, 1999. And on May 12, 1999, a masked gunman robbed an armoured car outside the Safeway store at Mountain Avenue and McGregor Street. Police say the robber has planned the heists well in advance. For instance, he's picked a time to act when he thinks it's the least anticipated and that the robberies are all in daylight and always in places full of people. He also knows when the armoured truck will be there and knows the layout of his getaway, leaving a stolen car in place hours beforehand. But what has police most concerned is the level of violence and his disregard for life." Syrnyk chuckled to himself about a police quote that said, *"it's possible the robbery yesterday was pulled by someone copying the method of operation used in the previous stickups."* Syrnyk had clearly hit the big time, the thought that other criminals might want to emulate him giving his already over-sized ego another boost.

● ● ● ● ● ●

"My car was hit with a bullet." The 41-year-old man had called police the day after the Safeway robbery, reporting yet another case of an innocent bystander narrowly avoiding tragedy during the wild, daytime shootout. This victim worked as a manager at a nearby bank and told investigators he didn't immediately check his 1997 Chrysler Intrepid the previous day because it was boxed in by police tape. Only in the late evening, when he was allowed to get the car out of the scene, did he discover a dent and chipped paint on the rear right fender. Police returned to the grocery store parking lot and began an additional search for evidence in the area where the man was parked. Only a few paint chips were found. No bullet was recovered, but police believed a shot had probably hit his fender, then ricocheted into the air and away from the vehicle. Once again, police were left shaking their heads at the fact nobody had been killed.

Police struck out in their attempts to gain information about the getaway vehicle that was abandoned near the crime scene. Heavy pedestrian traffic in the area had made a dog search impossible, especially given the passage of time from when the van was likely dumped to when it was found. Police did find a set of fresh footprints leading out of the u-shaped bay where the vehicle was located, but they disappeared after cutting through the front yard of a home towards the front street. Homeowners in the area claim they didn't see the car getting dumped or anything else suspicious.

An anxious public was demanding answers, and Winnipeg police were in the difficult position of being able to offer very little to settle the nerves of merchants, guards and innocent civilians worried they might be caught in the next crossfire. A few tips had come in, but nothing that appeared to be of substance or were related to the identity of the Yuletide Bandit. Inspector Keith McCaskill, the head of the major crimes unit, spoke publicly with the media the day following the Safeway incident, assuring all citizens that steps were being taken to bring the culprit to justice. He chose his words carefully, knowing it was likely the bandit was listening. McCaskill said extra officers would be assigned to work the case, but admitted police still hadn't identified a suspect. And he repeated a plea for public assistance, urging anyone with information to call immediately, even anonymously. Police braced for another onslaught of bogus leads and wasted time, but it was a necessary evil when you had little else to work with. Investigators didn't want to appear desperate, but behind the scenes, far away from the microphones and television cameras, they most certainly were.

••••••

Syrnyk was introduced to the young Frenchman through a mutual friend, a fellow cocaine user who also supplied the powder when needed. The stranger introduced himself as Rene Sylvestre. While snorting powder together, Syrnyk and Rene bonded quickly. Cocaine was taking Syrnyk out of his self-imposed shell, and he began enjoying the company of his fresh-faced new acquaintance. In a heavy French accent, Rene told Syrnyk plenty about his life. He came from a good French-Canadian family. Both his parents were alive and well and living in Winnipeg. He had a brother and sister he cared for deeply. There were many other relatives, including grandparents, aunts, uncles and cousins. The Sylvestre clan was tight. But Rene had separated himself from his loving family in recent months, an experiment with cocaine turning into an addiction that quickly got out of control. Rene was sucked into a wild party lifestyle – endless nights filled with a cocktail of alcohol, cocaine and women. Syrnyk took Rene under his wing, a protégé of sorts he enjoyed showing around town.

There was one major problem for Rene – living the so-called good life carried a heavy price tag. He quickly found himself out of cash and with no immediate prospect of income, as days were spent coming down off the previous night's high and getting ready for the next flight. Syrnyk wanted to help his friend. He enjoyed having someone around to talk to, someone who shared a common interest, and Syrnyk didn't want to lose his connection. One night, while both men were in a drug-induced frenzy, Syrnyk told Rene he could help him get some money. "But first you're going to have to pass a test," said Syrnyk.

● ● ● ● ● ●

March 1, 2002

The S.I.R. Sports Store on Ellice Avenue had been hit again. A middle-aged male clerk described to police a frightening scene that began when two masked men stormed into the store just before 9 p.m.. Both men were carrying shotguns. The pair ran directly to the rear gun counter, passing by about a dozen customers and staff members. Three young children were among the witnesses. "I was in an aisle and saw the two individuals. As soon as I saw them I assumed they were going for the guns. My priority was to confirm that others were calm and out of the way. I did not see them grab the guns, but on the return trip they had several guns in their arms," the clerk told investigators. "On their way out, one individual shouted out 'Yeah, fuck you!' to nobody in particular." He described the men as wearing dark clothing with either grey masks or duct tape covering their faces. Three shotguns, valued at approximately $2,500, were stolen. "How long were they in the store?" an officer asked the clerk. "About 30 seconds. They didn't stop. They seemed to know where they were going," he replied. Major crime investigators were immediately notified by general patrol officers about the hold-up. The general description and modus operandi suggested it was likely the work of the Yuletide Bandit. But a greater mystery to police was the sudden emergence of a second suspect.

The "test" turned out to be much more than Rene had bargained for. For a man with no previous brushes with the law, running into a crowded store waving a shotgun around was a jarring crash-course in the criminal lifestyle. Syrnyk told his friend the job had gone perfectly. He felt alive having someone along for the adventure and once again was having visions of forming an invincible team. He was lonely, and felt like he'd finally found someone who understood him. Rene, however, wasn't so sure. His conscience – when it wasn't clouded by crack – seemed to get the better of him, telling him he was on the path to destruction. To Syrnyk's chagrin, his partner in crime was calling it quits after one wonderful night. Syrnyk was alone again.

●●●●●●

During his many sexual escapades, Syrnyk met women from various walks of life. Some were loving mothers. Some were reckless drug addicts. Most were victims of some kind. And then there were the entrepreneurs. Syrnyk admired people who got creative in trying to make a buck, and his ability to get money whenever he needed it allowed him to lend a helping hand from time to time. One woman's venture was of particular interest to Syrnyk. Internet pornography.

Syrnyk first met the woman years earlier at a massage parlour and stayed in semi-regular contact, knowing she was struggling to make ends meet while supporting her children as a single mother. She made decent money selling sex, but the woman had expensive habits and needed more. The woman quietly set up a home-based website, catering to the crude and curious by offering links to various amateur pornography sites. She did most of her work while her children were in school, in bed, or with relatives. Her stay-at-home job was a secret to her family. Financial success was limited, as the World Wide Web offered millions of options for advertisers and everyone wanted their piece of the pie. Syrnyk was intrigued when the woman mentioned a possible "expansion" of her business, one she believed would allow her to stand out in cyberspace and create a cash windfall. She wanted to begin creating her own pornography, broadcasting video-on-demand into the homes of Internet browsers willing to pay a few extra bucks for a "personal touch." Trouble is, the woman needed some additional video equipment that was bound to be expensive. Her daily cash flow limited her options. Syrnyk suggested he might be able to help.

• • • • • •

March 21, 2002

The sight of a masked man wielding an axe was a truly terrifying sight for customers inside the Future Shop store in Winnipeg's St. James neighbourhood, just across the street from Polo Park Shopping Centre. He had burst into the store just before closing time, carrying a green garbage pail in his hands. The man set the pail on the floor and immediately pulled out a shotgun, screaming at everyone not to move. A large man who was shopping in the store took a few steps towards the gunman.

A coked-up Syrnyk raised the shotgun, pointing it directly at the man, and prepared to shoot. The shotgun was loaded but hadn't been chambered, but Syrnyk quickly fixed that with a "click" which seemed to convey to the wannabe hero that he meant business. The man stepped back, reluctantly raising his arms in the air. Syrnyk could see the intense anger in his eyes. The gun still in hand, Syrnyk again pulled the axe out of the garbage pail. He moved towards a glass display counter housing several digital cameras and web cams, reached back with the weapon and gave a mighty swing. Pieces of shattered glass fell in all directions, the violent move striking further anxiety in customers who feared for their lives. Syrnyk reached into the case and scooped up several cameras, dropping them into his garbage pail. He fled the store, but not before pointing the gun again in the direction of several customers who were still frozen with fear. A routine evening trip to a popular electronics store had turned into a nightmare they would never forget.

Syrnyk's friend was thrilled with the gift. Several cameras were ready to start recording lurid, homemade images that would be broadcast around the world. Syrnyk was happy to help. He had a much more personal motive for hitting the Future Shop. Reading about his crimes lately had given Syrnyk a new kind of rush, a surge of power in knowing that his actions had caused such a ripple effect in the community. Daily cocaine use was causing Syrnyk to have extreme fantasies about how to increase that coverage, to make sure everyone in Manitoba, even Canada, would know about him. He had come up with a brilliant idea. What if, instead of just reading about his crimes, people could actually see them as they happened? As in up close and personal.

Syrnyk wanted to begin wearing a small pinhole camera on his body, which would record a first-hand perspective of his crimes in progress. He hadn't found one during the frantic Future Shop hold-up, but paid a return visit to the Spy Shop he had robbed years earlier. Only this time he was a law-abiding customer. Pumped with cocaine, Syrnyk found just what he was looking for and returned home to play with his new toy. He planned to test it out soon, and then send the raw footage to local television stations. Producers would surely wet themselves at the juicy video they'd been delivered on a silver platter. Can you say ratings?

• • • • • •

Spring was in the air. Snow was melting quickly, and the warm weather was bringing Manitobans out of their winter hibernation and back on to the street. Syrnyk wasn't taking any time to savour the dawn of a new season. He couldn't have cared less. Walking quickly and with a purpose, Syrnyk set out from his West End Winnipeg home, headed towards downtown. His feet led him into a large Anglican church, located in the heart of the city just across from the Eaton's shopping centre. Syrnyk walked through the large gated entrance, through the front doors and quickly took a seat in one of the front pews. It was mid-day, and the parish was empty.

Syrnyk could hear the voices of a couple of elderly women in one of the back rooms, but couldn't see them. He fidgeted in his seat, contemplating his next move. He was sweating now, his hands wet with anxiety. Syrnyk had thought for days about this moment, about escaping the world he'd created for himself in the most hallowed of places. Gone were his mother, his family, and the friends he could have had. His life had become nothing more then a miserable existence filled with drugs and despair. Gone was hope.

Syrnyk had always felt comfort in the church. He thought it would be the perfect place to end his life. Syrnyk wanted to shoot one bullet in the palm of his hand. He'd fire another two into his feet. The pain would surely be excruciating, but Syrnyk wanted to feel every second of it. When it became too much, he would calmly raise the gun to his head and pull the trigger. Syrnyk cast another glance around the church, ensuring he was still alone. Then he pulled the gun from his pocket.

CHAPTER 18

April 7, 2002

Churches had emptied out, which meant the beginning of another devout practice for many Winnipeggers – Sunday shopping. The parking lot at the Safeway store on Jefferson Avenue and McPhillips Street had quickly filled up in the hour since the grocery goliath had opened for the day. Men in dark suits and sweaters, women in pretty spring dresses and slacks, and children fidgeting in their stuffy formalwear were coming in by the dozens. They carefully moved out of the way as a large Securicor truck came rolling by.

Richard Long, a 25 year veteran with the Canadian Forces, had started working for the armoured car company two years ago. He stepped from the passenger side of the truck while his partner, Serge Lechance, remained behind the wheel. Long grabbed a large bag of coins and headed inside Safeway. It was business as usual, with Long quickly handing over the coins in exchange for two bags of cash. One bag was from the store, the other from the gas bar located just outside in the parking lot. "I'm coming back out," Long said into his two-way radio as he began walking towards the doors. "Okay, looks good," Lechance replied from the truck outside.

Long paused as he reached the front entrance, just enough time to take a quick scan of the parking lot. All looked well. He continued through the doors, only to hear what sounded like someone shouting. Long couldn't make out the words. Then he heard the gunshot – and felt the burn of a shotgun slug graze his ear.

James VanSanten was headed towards the grocery store entrance when the crack of gunfire erupted in the parking lot. Unlike other customers, scurrying to safety wasn't as easy as diving to the ground or ducking behind a car. VanSanten was stuck in his electric wheelchair. He turned his head at the sound of the blast to see a man wearing a balaclava, standing maybe 10 feet directly behind him. VanSanten's eyes quickly moved to the shotgun, which appeared to be pointing directly at him. In fact, the gun was pointed at the armoured car guard who had emerged from the store, directly behind him. The guard reached for his gun and started firing. VanSanten was caught directly in the middle.

Long didn't hesitate in grabbing his revolver and returning fire. He squeezed the trigger hard, firing round after round after round. He dropped the money bags to the ground, freeing up both hands. Long could see the masked bandit crouched down, still firing his shotgun. The man's feet were sidestepping, the way members of a SWAT team would move. He could also see a terrified man in a wheelchair scrambling to get out of the way.

Shoppers were screaming and ducking for cover, some behind their own cars and others dropping directly to the pavement. Many ran back into the store. Long felt another shot graze his chest, which was covered with a bullet-proof vest that he'd paid for out of his own pocket. He'd complained about the $800 expense at the time, but it probably just saved his life.

Long's revolver was empty. All six rounds had been fired. "Shit," he shouted. Long retreated, taking cover behind a pillar at the front of the store. His hands trembled as he opened up the gun and re-loaded. He thought of his wife and two young children, praying he was going to live to see them again. With the gun again ready for battle, Long searched for the bandit, who had stopped firing. Turns out his partner had taken up the chase.

Lechance threw the Securicor truck into reverse as soon as he heard the shots ring out.

He knew Long was in trouble. Lechance watched as the bandit grabbed the money bags while Long retreated and reloaded, moving directly into the path of the truck. Lechance stepped hard on the gas. The bandit jumped out of the way, just as Lechance was about to run him over. He began running through the parking lot, stopping at a blue Dodge Caravan parked

Mike McIntyre

nearby in a handicapped spot. The man got inside. Lechance turned his truck around and moved towards the getaway vehicle. The sliding passenger door was still open as it began to drive away. Once again, Lechance took aim at the bandit. He drove his truck directly into the side, the impact jolting him back in his seat. The passenger door was completely shorn off. The bandit kept going. And so did Lechance.

•••••

Michael Syrnyk couldn't believe what was happening. This madman was actually chasing him. He'd planned this heist out meticulously, more than any of his previous ones, and couldn't believe it had gone so wrong. Five times he'd set his stolen cars up and waited to pounce, only to change his mind because the conditions just weren't right. Too much traffic. Police officers in the area. Too many pedestrians. Bad weather. But today had seemed like the perfect day.

In many ways, it still was. Syrnyk was enjoying the thrill of the chase, thanks to the heavy doses of crack cocaine that had become part of his everyday experience in the past few months. He no longer valued his life or the lives of others. Syrnyk had been within a heartbeat of killing himself just weeks earlier, but couldn't find the courage to pull the trigger inside the church. He wasn't ready to die, at least not yet, deciding at the last instance he still had some fight left in him.

Syrnyk sped through the parking lot in his damaged van, the sounds of gunshots still ringing in

224

his ears. Syrnyk had planned to ambush the guards as he sat inside the back of his van for nearly half-an-hour, covered by a dark tarp, waiting for them to arrive. But the element of surprise no longer seemed effective, as all guards seemed to almost be waiting for his arrival. They were pulling their guns out immediately, and Syrnyk felt like he had no choice but to begin shooting.

A trail of leaking anti-freeze and a pile of scattered broken car parts were being left behind in the parking lot. Syrnyk turned west on Jefferson Avenue, driving a few blocks before heading down a residential street. He could see the armoured truck directly behind him in the rear-view mirror. He couldn't believe the guy was able to move so fast. Syrnyk stepped on the gas, trying not to lose control of the van but attempting to put some distance between them. But the truck was getting closer. Syrnyk's speed was approaching 80 kilometres per hour, but he was losing ground. Syrnyk didn't know how much more damage his van could sustain.

In a split-second, Syrnyk jumped the curb of a home on Martindale Place, stopping in the front yard. A handful of residents from the home were just pulling out of their driveway at that exact moment. The Securicor truck smashed into his van once again, knocking a startled Syrnyk to the side. He tried to throw the van into reverse, but it wouldn't budge. Syrnyk jumped out, grabbing the cash bags. He ran towards the garage, realizing he'd left his shotgun inside the van. With the armoured car driver still inside his truck, Syrnyk took a big risk in running back to the van to retrieve his gun. He then headed back towards the garage and jumped a fence. There was another getaway car waiting nearby.

The bandit had made off with $31,000, but nobody who'd just been involved in the Sunday afternoon horror show cared about the cash. "I'm just shaking," said one man, who had just left Safeway when the violence erupted. As he sat in his wheelchair, VanSanten lit up a cigarette while trying to slow his racing heart and explain to police what he'd just witnessed. "I don't know what I was feeling. I just didn't want to get hit. I just got out of the way," he said. "If I'd been standing at his level, I'd have been killed." VanSanten told police he had quit smoking nine months ago. "This was a good reason to start again," he joked.

A least 10 shots had been exchanged between the two men, according to Winnipeg police identification officers. Two parked cars, fortunately with nobody inside, had been hit in the crossfire by wayward shots. Long told police he thought he hit the gunman but that it didn't appear the man was wounded. How somebody wasn't injured or killed during the Sunday afternoon shoot-out was beyond explanation. It was another miracle.

• • • • • •

The Yuletide Bandit

"I'm just shaking," witness Brian Vanderlip told the *Winnipeg Free Press*. "They have to get this fool before someone really gets hurt."

Faced with growing anxiety and concern from terrified Winnipeggers, justice officials moved fast to show they were responding. Police, the provincial justice department and Securicor all ordered reviews of the shootout on April 9. Winnipeg police Insp. Jack Tinsley was tasked with leading the city probe, which would examine the licencing and training of armoured-car guards. "Retaliation fire is the concern. How do these incidents escalate to gunfire and how is it returned?" said Tinsley. "This is extremely serious. And a man in a wheelchair was caught in the centre." Major crimes Inspector Keith McCaskill once again tried to re-assure the public they were on the case and doing their best to find the bandit. But it was getting more difficult with each unsolved crime to make the case.

Police agencies from across Canada were calling city investigators to offer assistance, but there was little they could do. A similar criminal pattern didn't exist anywhere in Canada, which likely suggested their man was a local product. Police admitted publicly they were frustrated more solid leads and tips hadn't poured in. They were also puzzled by what appeared to be a change in behaviour. After several Christmas heists, the bandit had now hit two Safeway stores in as many months. One police official compared their elusive Yuletide Bandit to Ken Leishman, Winnipeg's infamous "Flying Bandit", who robbed banks across Canada in the 1950s by flying to various cities. In 1966, Leishman pulled off the biggest cold robbery in Canadian history at the Winnipeg International Airport. Ironically, Leishman met his maker in a plane crash years later.

Tinsley continued to question the role of armoured car guards, noting that city police officers have to qualify twice a year at the gun range to be able to carry a sidearm. If they fail, they must go for re-training. The average pass mark by officers in re-qualifying is 93 per cent, usually by hitting 43 or 44 out of 45 stationary targets. "The private security firms are nowhere near that," said Tinsley. He said police are trained to only fire their weapons when they're confident there is no other option. Guards should drop the money and run, and not reach for their weapons, when confronted by a robber. "Even if you're under heavy fire, you can't return fire unless it's safe. You seek cover," he said. "Drop the bag. It's just money."

Ross Parry, the spokesman for Securicor, said his company would review both the incident and the guards' general training and procedures. "We're coming to the conclusion in Winnipeg, obviously, we're on to the same person, some sort of serial bandit robber. We have to heighten our focus, our anticipation, our preparation," he said. "He's a very persistent criminal, with very extreme levels of risk. It's virtually unprecedented."

The Yuletide Bandit

Gord Mackintosh, the provincial NDP justice minister, also waded into the fray by ordering his department to review the Sunday afternoon shooting spree. "This is about the public safety of Manitobans," he said. "Security guards are on the front line of public safety. We want to get a firm understanding of the regulations governing this sector, this industry, to see if there are gaps that pose a risk to the guards and the public." Several other so-called "experts" weighed in with their opinions. Harry Lazarenko, a long-time Winnipeg city councillor, predicted somebody would soon be killed. "We've got a problem. If daylight robberies like this can take place, we're going back to the days of Wild Bill Hickock and Jesse James," he said. Lazarenko said guards should use more caution when making pickups and deposits. Randy Terpstra, a former police officer who provides security training for guards in Minnesota, claimed Long and Lechance put innocent lives at risk. "These guards are armed to protect their lives and the lives of people around them. They are trained to use deadly force only if lives are in danger. But in this case, the bag of money had been relinquished and the guy was fleeing," he said. "My reaction to this is they were out of line."

Long reached his breaking point when he picked up the newspaper the morning of April 10. After reading a seemingly endless stream of criticism, Long broke his silence by agreeing to an exclusive interview with Bruce Owen, the crime reporter for the *Winnipeg Free Press*. Long told Owen it was ridiculous that senior police officials, the province and Securicor had all launched investigations into the conduct of himself and Lechance. "All these guys can yap as much as they want, but until they're put in my boots, they should stay quiet," said a defiant Long. He believed his life was at risk and that he relied on his guard training, which was to empty their handguns quickly at a hostile moving target by firing six rounds at close range in under nine seconds. And you never, ever give up your gun. "You've got to make a decision like this in a heartbeat. You've also got to be willing to take a bullet if a little old lady is standing in front of you," said Long. He defied police to put themselves in his position and still criticize his actions. "The gunman dictated what was going to happen. He didn't give an option. I've gone over this a thousand times in my mind and I couldn't have done anything different," he said. "He damn near killed me." Long said armoured car guards should be paid better than your average convenience store clerk. He was making $8.50 after six months of service. "A guy at 7-Eleven makes that, and here I am carrying around a gun," he said. "I've become the scapegoat for doing my job. I'm the bad guy, and that's not right." He had already been told to stay off work indefinitely, until a psychologist deemed him fit to return. "They want to make sure I'm not sitting in the bathroom with a gun in my mouth," Long told friends.

Long's rebuttal to his critics was front-page news, his angry face, dramatic story and bold statements greeting tens of thousands of Manitobans the morning of April 11. Charles Adler, the popular, hard-nosed morning talk-show host on Winnipeg's top-ranked radio station, CJOB, was flooded with phone calls from listeners wanting to voice support for Long. "It was enormous. Everyone put themselves in his position. They think he did the right thing and that he shouldn't be second-guessed," Adler told the media following the conclusion of his show. Other guards, both working and retired, also rallied around Long. Lloyd Stacey, who no longer worked in the profession, sent Long a supportive e-mail. "Mr. Long, you did just fine. You and your peers know that in the vast majority of heists, 90 percent of the fatalities occur in the first 10 seconds, and usually it's the guard who gets hit. If you feel like you let the community down, go hug your kids, and remember that you came home," Stacey wrote.

Mackintosh read the newspaper and realized he'd put himself as the centre of a political firestorm with his comments that appeared to criticize Long's actions. He phoned the embattled guard the morning of April. 11, catching Long as he prepared to be interviewed by several television stations eager to follow the hot story. Mackintosh said he wanted to personally let Long know he supported him and never intended to undermine the reality of the dangerous job he had. Long accepted the apology. He also took the opportunity to call on Mackintosh to order armoured car companies to provide all guards with bullet-proof vests and better firearms. "If I had an automatic, I would've got him. If I killed him, everything would be different. Instead I'm being criticized. I go from a hero to a chump," said Long.

The union representing security guards waded into the debate, calling on the federal government to make it mandatory for armoured car companies to use three guards at all time and ensure adequate firearms training. "The way this bandit operates, his motivation is to kill the guards," union leader Rich Ashdown told reporters. Mackintosh vowed the issue would be explored in the provincial review. "Security guards are on the front line of public safety. We want to get a firm understanding of the regulations governing this sector, this industry, to see if there are gaps that pose a risk to the guards and the public," Mackintosh said publicly.

The *Winnipeg Free Press* published a sampling of reader opinions in their letters section on April 16:

"During the recent armoured van robbery, my wife was one of the people near the front of the Safeway store with her groceries when the shooting started. Thank God she and others were not physically injured, although she was traumatized and had to hide, crouching behind packing crates until the incident was over. Having a gunman firing a shotgun in a public place is bad enough, but having an armed guard repeatedly fire his weapon in a wild west-styled shootout, while another rams and pursues the getaway van into a residential area where further shooting could have been triggered, is extremely disconcerting as well."

The Yuletide Bandit

Paul Moreau
Winnipeg

"I am astounded over the recent coverage regarding the incident that occurred at the Safeway location on McPhillips Street and Jefferson Avenue. I am even more baffled that Ross Parry, spokesman for Securicor, could not provide tangible information regarding training that Securicor employees receive. This not only leads me to believe that the company has no regard for its employees, but the public as well as he is clearly not "in tune" with the company or the industry. I also cannot understand why the federal and provincial governments have not stepped in to enact legislation regarding wages and training. I would assume that both levels of government understand that any losses as a result of hold-ups would be passed on to the consumers in one form or fashion. They must also realize that most employees will take "a bit more on the chin" if they are paid well for the work they do and in turn, lower the turnover experienced by the industry, which produces a more stable and trained workforce. I do not personally believe that these guards exercised poor judgment as most people have a good understanding of right from wrong actions. For this they should be commended and not persecuted."

Eugene Cvitan
Winnipeg

Securicor quickly finished its review of Long and Lechance's actions in an attempt to stave off any more bad publicity. Parry, the company spokesman, said his company found guards followed all procedures and even went beyond the call of duty to defend themselves and protect others from harm. "It is the company's view that the actions of Richard Long and Serge Lechance at the scene of the crime demonstrated sound and proper judgment. We believe that the use of force, in this case the discharging of a firearm, was both justified and undertaken in a judicious manner," said Parry. "By attempting to halt the suspect's escape from the scene of the crime, our employees displayed alert and reasonable judgment and considerable bravery to apprehend a suspect that clearly posed a continued threat to them and to the public." Securicor was studying several safety improvements in the wake of the latest attack, Parry announced. The company would review adding a third person to routes with large cash pick-ups that are deemed high-risk. Securicor would also begin varying their routes and schedules, hoping to throw the Yuletide Bandit off from establishing a set pattern. Mandatory bullet-proof vests and greater firepower – perhaps semi-automatic pistols – would also be studied, Parry promised. "This is an aberration. People don't normally knock over an armoured car by shooting first. But here you've got a guy who opens fire first and asks questions later," he said. Parry noted there were more armoured car heists in Winnipeg during the past two years than the rest of Canada combined over the last five years. With the company fully behind them, Long and Lechance had one less thing to worry about.

The Yuletide Bandit

Could money talk? Winnipeg's Crime Stoppers certainly hoped so as they quickly doubled their normal cash award for information leading to the arrest of the Yuletide Bandit. Wade Doberstein, the police coordinator of the program, promised $2,000 to the successful tipster. "Someone is going to get hurt, badly, and we'd like to put this thing to rest as quickly as possible," Doberstein told the public during a news conference. "Maybe someone out there knows something, but they're scared because they think they have to deal with police. We can take the information and it will be completely anonymous." Long heard about the financial bait on the news and wished it was higher. But he prayed someone would quickly come forward. "I know he's going to strike again, probably in the next couple of months," he told a friend. "Obviously, this guy has no regard for his own life and he doesn't care about anyone else's."

CHAPTER 19

The Kevlar vest was slung over a chair as Michael Syrnyk raised his Polaroid instant camera to eye level and clicked twice. Two perfect pictures emerged seconds later, both showing the body armour in clear detail. Syrnyk set the images aside, then sat down in front of an old typewriter that was still kicking around his family's St. James home. His dad had moved into the home with Syrnyk shortly after Virginia Syrnyk's death. Syrnyk used one finger at a time to strike the keys, being careful not to make any mistakes. He was sober, his thoughts clear and concise. Syrnyk began the letter by addressing it to the armoured car companies of Winnipeg. "Obviously I am not screwing around here. I am the criminal. You are the company. Somebody is going to get killed here," he slowly typed.

Syrnyk was still rattled by the Safeway mess, angered how the guards went on the offensive and nearly ran him down after nearly taking him out with a bullet. This was not the way he wanted to operate. Syrnyk felt it was time to send a clear message that he wasn't fooling around, and that guards should just drop the money and freeze next time he shows up on the scene. It would be easier for everyone. "Take your losses, or somebody's going to get shot here," Syrnyk continued typing. He helpfully pointed out that large businesses have insurance, so why all the fuss over money they didn't really stand to lose anyways? "I'm not here for a gunfight. I don't want to shoot anyone. This vest protects me head to toe." Syrnyk figured most guards knew he was covered by armour anyways, so he wasn't giving away a trade secret by openly boasting about it. But perhaps it would send a wake-up call to guards who seemed to be getting trigger-happy. Syrnyk tried to play on the company's civic responsibilities by telling them it wouldn't look good to have the blood of an innocent bystander on their hands. "I'm not going to back down. So why don't you tell your guys to back down. Just lie down, prone, and I'll take the money and run," he typed. Syrnyk placed the letter in an envelope, including the two snapshots of his vest.

The Safeway robbery had been Syrnyk's most frightening experience to date, even outdoing the Polo Park mayhem. He was getting closer to being caught, or killed, and Syrnyk knew he was running out of chances. In the weeks preceding the Safeway attack, Syrnyk's paranoia caused him to pack a shotgun for the first time while he walked the streets of Winnipeg looking for cars to steal in preparation for his next strike. He was carrying at least 20 rounds with him at all times. Syrnyk worried police would catch him in the act one of these days, and he wanted to be ready for the inevitable encounter. Police had his DNA, and Syrnyk would never go willingly. It might just be a simple car theft charge, but once they took him for fingerprinting, it would all be over. So Syrnyk planned to go down fighting, if necessary. Luckily for everyone, he had yet to be caught in the act of stealing a car.

Syrnyk was beginning to think about his next move, not wanting to spend too much time dwelling on everything that had gone wrong. Given recent events, he was pondering a switch back to night-time heists, when less pedestrians and motorists would be around and it just boiled down to a showdown between the guards and him. Syrnyk's head was filled with ideas from all the reading he'd done on storied robberies of the past, and he was eager to try out something new, something dramatic. His pinhole camera was ready to go, and Syrnyk planned to videotape his next crime and let Manitobans see it happen through his eyes. The element of surprise was always crucial, and Syrnyk felt it would be to his benefit to hide out on the roof of a bank, clutching a rope that would be tied down to something secure in the area. As the guards left the branch with the full bags of money, Syrnyk could swoop down like some kind of superhero, landing on his feet, of course. He would already be clutching his gun, and the guards would likely be so stunned by his surprise grand entrance they'd have no time to react with their own weapons. It sounded like the perfect plan.

• • • • • •

Megan Ireland didn't take any crap. The short, stocky, tough-as-nails blonde had been on the receiving end of some of life's cruellest blows, yet she was still standing, her pride still very much intact. Her worn face, broken-down body and wealth of street smarts gave the appearance of someone much older then her 24 years suggested. The crude tattoo on Megan's leg probably best summed up her view on life – "Fuck You". Megan had been permanently branded at a wild house party years earlier, after she passed out from drugs and alcohol. That night was one of many in her recent past that were a foggy blur, a series of addictions taking over her life. Megan had moved from British Columbia 10 months earlier, settling on Winnipeg for a fresh start.

Megan quickly landed a job at Club 205, a small but successful massage parlour situated in Winnipeg's Chinatown district. It was safer than selling her body on the streets, something she had done in the past. Her office was on the third-floor of an old brick building, above a popular travel agency, and just down the street from Winnipeg's City Hall and Public Safety Building where city police were headquartered. Club 205 was also near the heart of the city's bar and theatre district, which was a major boon for its late-night business. Megan was one of several young, female massage therapists, but her duties went well beyond rubbing the knotty backs of her clientele. Usually, the massage was just foreplay, a prelude to what her customers really wanted from her – sex. Megan tolerated the degrading work, which made her decent money and even better connections in the city's drug culture, where most of her profits were spent. And so the vicious cycle continued.

The dishevelled man was wearing a brown leather jacket when he walked into Club 205 and ordered the full treatment. Megan took the client to a private room in the back of the building. He was grungy, and appeared quite disturbed. Megan was nervous but not worried, as many of her customers weren't exactly in peak condition. Megan briefly described her services and rates with the shabby stranger, and the pair got down to business. Megan sensed the man was a regular but asked him few questions. After all, most customers weren't paying for idle chit-chat. The man also said very little, and hardly made an impression in thefew moments Megan spent with him. He got dressed and left without so much as a good-bye.

Megan's shift was over, another night of high risks and low returns. She walked down three flights of stairs and headed outside. Standing just outside the front doors was the man with the brown leather jacket.

● ● ● ● ● ●

There was something about the woman that had Syrnyk curious to know more. When they were alone together in the room, he noticed something most peculiar about her. A third nipple. Syrnyk once read something about the unusual body marking which suggested third nipples represent psychic abilities. He didn't say anything during the act, keeping quiet as he always did. But Syrnyk couldn't stop thinking about the woman in the few minutes since he'd left the massage parlour. Syrnyk was feeling especially lonely tonight, his cocaine high wearing off. He was thinking about Marlene, her children, and what could have been. How he had messed everything up, thrown away the one good chance he had for a happy life. Syrnyk longed for some stability in his life, but knew he would always prevent it from happening. So he would seek out other people just like him, people who were emotionally empty. People like Megan.

"Do you want to maybe get a coffee or something?" a nervous Syrnyk asked Megan as the pair stood under a streetlight on Winnipeg's Main Street, just outside the massage parlour. The woman seemed taken aback by his question. Megan wasn't adverse to seeing customers outside of work, especially if it meant scoring some drugs. But she sensed something different about this man. After some idle chit-chat, Megan suggested they get in a cab and go to a Portage Avenue café called the Chocolate Shop. There couldn't be any harm in a friendly little drink, she figured.

"What do you do?" Syrnyk wasn't prepared for the question, which Megan tossed at him shortly after they sat down in a booth. He couldn't remember the last time anyone had ever asked him that. Megan – who claimed she was clairvoyant – broke the silence by making her best guess. "I see a bank," she said. Syrnyk was stunned. "No comment," he said with a forced chuckle. He studied Megan closely for her reaction, and was relieved when she laughed too. Syrnyk quickly changed the conversation. He mentioned the third nipple and leg tattoo he'd seen on Megan. She mentioned the two triangles on his arms.

They chatted well into the night, each slowly letting down their guard. Cigarette butts were piling up in the ashtray. Syrnyk talked about his interest in books and his lack of a social or family life. Megan spoke of her troubled life on the west coast, and her loneliness since coming to Winnipeg. Syrnyk brought the subject of religion, and God, into the discussion. He told Megan of trying to speak with God in his worst moments, but getting no response. He felt empty. So did she. Both spoke about their reliance on drugs to mask their pain. Megan, of course, knew plenty of dealers who supplied quality cocaine. She promised to hook Syrnyk up. Syrnyk said the price didn't matter – he was willing to pay whatever it took. The night ended with the pair exchanging phone numbers and promising to meet again soon. Syrnyk loved the way she had listened to him. Megan was intrigued at the man beneath the rough exterior. Both were interested in drugs. It was the start of a fateful relationship.

• • • • • •

Syrnyk and Megan were sitting together in the living room of her tiny downtown apartment block, having just smoked their last ounce of crack cocaine. Both were in a heightened state of awareness and edginess. Syrnyk had fallen hard for Megan in just the few short days since they'd met. He saw a potential partnership together.

"What would you think about helping me steal a car?" Syrnyk blurted out. The question knocked Megan for a loop.

"Are you serious?" she said.

"Yeah. The two of us, it would be really romantic," said Syrnyk. Megan just laughed. Syrnyk stood up, and walked towards a duffel bag he'd brought to Megan's place when she first invited him to sleep over a couple nights earlier. He unzipped the bag and pulled out his Kevlar vest. Syrnyk proudly held it up for Megan to see. The cocaine had knocked him silly, and Syrnyk figured he no longer had anything to lose.

"You know the guy that's been going around robbing armoured cars? That's me. I'm the guy the papers are writing about," he said proudly. The secret was out – and Syrnyk couldn't have cared less. Megan had no idea what he was talking about. It had been a long time since she followed the news. She managed another laugh, chalking Syrnyk's ramblings to some drug-induced bravado. His expression was dead serious. "I do it for the adrenaline rush," he continued. Syrnyk said he started by doing banks, but that he didn't like to victimize women so he switched over to armoured cars. "It's easier to rob guys than women," he said. Syrnyk could see doubt in Megan's eyes, and perhaps a little bit of fear. He could tell she was uncomfortable, so he dropped the discussion for the time being. It felt great to finally tell someone other than Rene the coward, who clearly wasn't cut out for the criminal lifestyle.

Megan solved the cocaine crisis with a couple quick phone calls. "A couple of friends are on the way," she told Syrnyk, who had fallen asleep on the couch. His high had worn off, and Syrnyk was suddenly feeling agitated and jumpy, now very much aware of the fact he'd told Megan everything. What had he done? How could he have been so careless? Syrnyk's heart began to race as he panicked, realizing a crack addict he'd just met days earlier now controlled his destiny. Syrnyk no longer had the power.

Two young men, Adam and Pedro, arrived in the early evening. Syrnyk was in no mood for company, but Megan had invited them over to score more drugs. All four sat down in the living room. Adam and Pedro began talking about their endless supply, their associates, and their weaponry. Syrnyk was doing a slow burn, the task of listening to these amateur shitheads becoming almost too much to handle. He wanted to get rid of them quickly, so he asked to see the cocaine. He told the men he wanted an ounce. "Where do you get all this money to buy this coke?" Adam asked, having made several deliveries to Megan in the past few days alone that were all financed by her new friend.

"Fuck, just whatever you got, I want," Syrnyk said tersely. Adam and Pedro continued to blather about their drugs and their guns to the point of excess. Syrnyk tried to hurry the deal along. "I hope you're not a narc," said Pedro in an accusatory tone. Syrnyk's rage exploded at the accusation he was working for the police. "Fuck, you guys wanna talk about guns and shit…Here's my gun," he said. Syrnyk reached into his pocket and pulled out his Glock nine-millimetre. He was pointing it directly towards Megan's two friends.

A hush fell over the room, with nobody moving an inch as Syrnyk brandished the weapon. Megan eventually broke the silence by screaming at Syrnyk to leave her apartment. The sight of the gun had truly frightened her to the point she thought that Syrnyk was either telling the truth about his criminal past, or was completely crazy. In any event, she'd seen enough. "You can't come here anymore," she said. Syrnyk put the gun away and was happy to oblige. Syrnyk grabbed his few belongings and fled out the door without saying another word.

● ● ● ● ● ●

The hours, and days, began to mount. Tension was eating away at Syrnyk like a cancer. A coke-sniffing hooker, who'd kicked him out of her house, now had the power to bring him down. Certainly, his little game of show-and-tell had only aggravated the situation. If Megan hadn't believed him at first, she must have serious questions now. Syrnyk picked up the phone and dialed her number. Megan's answering machine picked up. "We need to talk. Call me," Syrnyk said tersely. He slammed down the receiver.

In his darkest hour, Syrnyk reached out to the one woman he knew he could always trust. Marlene appeared genuinely happy to see him when he showed up at her door unannounced. It had been months since they last saw each other, and Syrnyk's surprise visit had come out of the blue to Marlene. Syrnyk was also given a jolt of his own. Marlene didn't have much time to talk, because she had to get to a medical appointment. It was at a fertility clinic. Marlene explained she'd found someone else, a new man in her life who shared her dream of having another baby. Only this time, Marlene wasn't going to take any chances. Doctors felt fertility treatment was the best way to go following her miscarriage. Syrnyk felt like a dagger had just been thrust through his heart.

The tears started flowing and Marlene pulled Syrnyk close to her for a warm embrace. Syrnyk wanted to kill himself on the spot, his often wavering will to live now completely gone. What a failure he was, in every way. Marlene finally let go, telling Syrnyk she was going to be late. Before she got in her vehicle, Syrnyk had one final request. He wanted a picture. Marlene reached into her purse and pulled out a snapshot of the two of them together, in happier times.

• • • • • •

May 1, 2002

Megan was about to begin another night of work at Club 205 when she heard what sounded like two angry voices coming from the stairwell. It was just before 6 p.m.. As she continued to walk up to the third floor, the voices got louder. Syrnyk was standing at the top of the staircase. He was alone.

Megan went cold. She had been avoiding Syrnyk's constant phone calls and messages for a couple days, suddenly afraid of a man she realized she didn't even know. Megan tried to walk by Syrnyk to get inside the office, but he reached his arm out and grabbed her. "We have to talk," Syrnyk said, his words slurring. Megan could see his eyes were blood red and glazed, with large, dark bags underneath. He was unshaven, greasy and somewhat wobbly on his feet.

"I can't believe how badly you've hurt me. How could anyone do this to me," Syrnyk continued.

"What do you mean," Megan said, fear evident in her voice. She again tried to get by him.

"You can't walk away from me," Syrnyk said, his tone more demanding and much louder. "We have to go somewhere and talk."

Megan forcefully said 'No', and struggled to escape his grip. The she noticed the shiny tip of a knife behind Syrnyk's back.

Megan tried to back away but found herself stuck between a wall and an angry Syrnyk. "You have a knife?" she asked, her eyes fixed on the shiny silver and black metal object behind his back.

"You know things about me. You know too much. You have to forget me," he said. Syrnyk reached back and threw the weapon – straight onto the ground. It bounced off the top stair, landing on its side. Megan quickly thrust her foot out to step on the knife, then bent down and picked it up. Syrnyk didn't seem to care.

"I just want to go, I just want to go to work," Megan pleaded, her hands trembling as she grasped the weapon. She carefully took a few small steps, positioning herself near the door that led into Club 205. Megan reached back to grab the door handle. A desperate Syrnyk lunged forward and struck Megan with a shoulder tackle, knocking her to the ground.

Syrnyk easily grabbed the knife back from Megan's hand while pinning her down. He wasn't particularly proud about striking a woman for the first time in his life, but felt he had no choice. He ordered Megan to stand up, holding the knife close to her. Syrnyk stood beside Megan and pushed her towards her office, opening the door and walking inside. She was sobbing loudly. "I'm going to finish this before somebody finishes me," Syrnyk said.

CHAPTER 20

"Everyone get out of the building." Michael Syrnyk announced his presence inside Club 205 with a thundering voice, still holding Megan in front of him with the knife at her back. Two female employees jumped at the sight of Megan being forced into the office by the man they recognized as one of their more loyal customers. It was every sex trade worker's worst nightmare. The women scrambled for safety, ducking out the door and hoping Megan would join them. She didn't. The women ran into a washroom, taking cover and using a cellular phone to dial 911. They told the operator there was a serious disturbance involving a disgruntled customer armed with a knife. The operator calmly assured the caller police were on their way.

• • • • • •

Constables Daryl Smuttell and Mark Philippot were just easing into their evening shift duties, driving police unit 103 through Winnipeg's downtown district. It had been a slow start to their shift, which ran until 2:30 a.m.. The pair was near the Public Safety

Building when a call came across their two-way radio system. "Any Division 11 unit to attend 205 Alexander Avenue, third floor, Club 205. Report of a dispute between a customer and employee. Customer is apparently armed with a knife. Several people still inside the building." Smuttell, a four-year veteran, and Philippot, the senior officer with five years on the job, immediately voiced their response. They arrived in less than five minutes, parking their cruiser car just west of the building. Two other officers, both street supervisors, were also at the scene. A young woman was waiting for police outside the building.

"He's still up there, with the knife," she said excitedly. The woman had dashed out of the building when the irate customer, whom she identified as "Mike", had stormed into her office. The officers asked for directions to the massage parlour. The woman pointed directly to the stairs, telling them to go straight up to the third floor. "That's where you'll find them." Philippot went first. Smuttell was right behind him, followed by the street supervisors. All the officers drew their guns.

Syrnyk nervously paced around the room as Megan sat on a chair, afraid to move. Syrnyk was mumbling to himself. "You're going to have to stay here, with me," he told Megan. Syrnyk pulled an old photograph out of his pocket, a smiling headshot of himself taken when he was about six years old that he had found while going through his mother's belongings after her death. He placed the picture on his knee and pulled a nine-millimetre Glock semi-automatic handgun from inside his jacket. A camouflage painted sawed-off pump action shotgun was already resting at his feet, it too having been concealed by his jacket. Syrnyk looked so innocent in the picture. He wanted it to be the last thing he saw before he ended his life.

Syrnyk was ready for a confrontation with the police. That is why he had come tonight. Syrnyk, fuelled by three straight days without sleep and a never-ending supply of cocaine, recognized he was a goner. Megan knew too much, and would surely sell him out. His desperate calls to her had gone unanswered. He felt the only thing left to do was to go out on his terms. Syrnyk wanted a public spectacle. "When I kill myself, I don't want your death on my conscience," Syrnyk told Megan.

Philippot reached the top of the stairs, which immediately spilled out into a long, narrow hallway. The only way to go was to the right. Philippot turned, and saw a scruffy looking man standing just outside one of the doors at the end of the hall. He was holding a knife in his hand. "Winnipeg police. Drop the knife!" Philippot yelled. He pointed his gun at the man.

The police were finally in his sights. But their prompt arrival had caught Syrnyk by surprise. He bolted at the sight of the officers and ran back into the massage parlour at the end of the hallway. Syrnyk slammed the large wooden door shut behind him, leaving himself and Megan alone inside once again. He went for his guns.

Philippot gave chase down the hall, reaching the door just seconds after it closed. Locked. Smuttell was just behind him, while the two street supervisors waited in the stairwell. Philippot could see into the room through a rectangular shaped window. He spotted a woman standing across the room, but saw no sign of the man who'd just run away. The woman looked scared.

"Open the door," Philippot yelled. The woman just shook her head and pointed. Philippot couldn't see what she was motioning at. Philippot felt he had no other choice – he began kicking the door as hard as he could. "Winnipeg police," he shouted. He gave the door a hard kick. It gave way a little bit near the handle. "Winnipeg police," he repeated in an even louder voice. Another kick. More movement. Philippot was holding his gun tightly in his left hand. He stood back and prepared for a third kick to the door. Then all hell broke loose.

• • • • • •

Syrnyk could see the silhouettes of two officers through the door window when he raised his shotgun and pulled the trigger. The glass exploded. Most of the debris flew into the hallway, although some remained inside the window frame or trickled inside the office. Syrnyk braced himself for return fire.

The Yuletide Bandit

Philippot felt like his face was on fire. Broken glass had flown towards his head, and the sharp, burning pain told him he was hurt. There had been no time to react, both Philippot and Smuttell coming under attack just seconds after seeing the man come around the corner of the office in a crouching position. It was as if a bomb had gone off.

The officers knew they had to find cover immediately. But there was only one way out. Smuttell was feeling a burning sensation in his shoulder as he reached the end of the hallway and dove headfirst down the stairwell, worried more gunfire was coming. He fell down several stairs. The two street supervisors who had followed Smuttell and Philippot into the building now helped Smuttell up and escorted him out of the building. "I've been shot," said Smuttell. It appeared Philippot was still inside the building.

Although there was no doubt he was hit, Smuttell didn't know the extent of the damage. Now wasn't the time to worry about that. Smuttell and the two street supervisors ran outside, careful to hug the east side of the building fearing the gunman might take aim at them from a third-floor window. They ran to the nearest building, a Chinese restaurant called the Kum Koon Garden. Police immediately called for as many back-up officers as possible and an ambulance. There was grave concern about the fate of Philippot.

Struggling to see through his glass and blood covered eyes, a dazed Philippot was desperate to find a safe place. He stumbled towards what appeared to be an office adjacent to where the gunshots had come from and immediately ducked inside. There wasn't much to the room – a Coke machine, a desk and a couple chairs. Nothing large to take cover behind. Philippot knew he was still vulnerable. He raised his hand to wipe the debris from his face, only to realize it too was covered in blood. Panic began to set in as Philippot worried he'd been shot and seriously injured. He quickly scanned his body, but couldn't find anything but cuts on his hands and face. Philippot grabbed his two-way radio and told dispatch he was wounded and trapped inside a building. The gunman was still on the loose.

There was chaos in Chinatown. Dozens of Winnipeg police officers from around the city raced to the scene, running red lights and stop signs, going against traffic down one-way streets and giving rush-hour drivers a real shock. The information was sketchy at best. Two officers wounded, including one likely trapped inside the building where the gunman was possibly holed up with a hostage. The first officers to arrive on scene grabbed their shotguns and began ushering people off the street and sealing off the area with yellow tape. They had to secure a safe perimeter. "Until we figure out what's going on, it's not safe, not even for the officers right now," a frantic uniformed cop told several pedestrians, who quickly retreated inside a downtown hotel for cover. Diners inside several Chinese restaurants were ordered to remain inside, all the doors locked for fear the gunman could have escaped the massage parlour and be on the loose. Winnipeg police Chief Jack Ewatski was immediately notified of the situation by senior officers and headed straight to the hospital, where Smuttell was being transported with a suspected gunshot wound to the shoulder. The emergency response unit – a volunteer unit comprised of police officers from within the service who have specialized tactical training – began to assemble with military-like efficiency. Some officers were already at work, while others had to scramble to the scene from home. Their mission was simple – getting a wounded Philippot out alive.

●●●●●●

Debbie Johnson was working the evening shift inside the Winnipeg Police communication centre. Her day was barely two hours old when she answered the 911 call of her life. A frantic woman on the other end identified herself as Megan Ireland. She was being held hostage by a gun-toting Michael Syrnyk, who had just shot two city police officers. The fate of two more lives was now partially resting in Johnson's hands.

"I'm not gonna hold your hand while you kill yourself. I don't want you to kill yourself," Johnson, 43, heard Megan say over the line. She said Syrnyk was putting a handgun to his own head, threatening to take his own life. "You're doing a great job, okay? Okay Megan?" Johnson said, trying to keep the young woman calm.

Syrnyk was growing agitated about the sea of blue he could see down on the street below. He was staring out the window, his eyes drifting away from the frantic gun-toting officers towards the bright sun that was already quite low in the west sky. Suddenly, his worries seemed to vanish. Syrnyk felt a sense of peace as he stared directly into the blinding light, unable to turn away.

"What's he doing now?" Johnson asked Megan, worried about several seconds of silence on the line.

"I don't understand. He wants me to leave but then he'll be mad if I leave. I can't, I can't, I'm so…" Megan said Syrnyk was doing a line of cocaine.

"You're not gonna get hurt, I'm gonna fuckin' die here," Syrnyk shouted, interrupting Megan. Johnson could hear the anger in his voice.

"You're not gonna die," Megan told him. Johnson asked Megan where the gun was. Syrnyk was angered by the question.

"With all your education I was still fuckin' smarter than you. Little white trash fuckin' lunatic. But I'm not a lunatic, you're gonna find that out," he shouted into the phone. "Mike?" said Johnson. Megan said she was still holding the phone. "Tell him that nobody's calling him a lunatic, okay?" said Johnson. Syrnyk continued to rant, and Johnson struggled to pick up his words. "Why does it matter if you're gonna blow your own head off?" Johnson heard Megan say. "Megan. Try not to make any references to him blowing his head off, okay? Cause it just might agitate him more to do it," said Johnson.

Syrnyk finally grabbed the phone from Megan. He wanted to deal directly with the 911 operator. "Are you gonna talk to me?" he asked. "Yeah, go ahead, Mike," Johnson said in her most reassuring voice.

"Well, I mean, I just…my whole life, I've just had it," he said.

"What do you mean by that?"

"Well, I went nuts as a fuckin' kid and nobody saw it and they just let me suffer. I couldn't even cope in society at all, so what did I have to do? It start off with fucking B&E's," said Syrnyk. Johnson was somewhat startled by his admission. Syrnyk continued talking. "Then stealing cars, robbing banks up to the fuckin' really cool shit. I thought they would pay off and I could just leave. But obviously…the fuckin' government will own our ass from birth to death," he said.

"Mike, what happened? What happened at the beginning?" asked Johnson. She knew it was good to keep him talking as much as possible.

"I wouldn't lie to you 'cause what do I have to hide at this point. So fuck it. I never struck a woman in my life, ever. I've been shot at by fuckin' guys with guns. Life isn't fair," said Syrnyk. Johnson tried to focus on the positive.

"Mike, everything that you've been through, if you have managed never to hit a female or a woman. That is honourable, do you know that?" she asked.

"I've fucked a lot of whores just to keep myself sane," said Syrnyk.

"Did it help you?" said Johnson.

"Oh yeah, it helped me," he said.

Johnson wanted to get Syrnyk to focus on the situation at hand, to control his anger about the wrongs in his life.

"Tell me what happened today," she said.

"Can I just ask you something? They're not going to storm the place? It's gonna be a mess. I don't want that, okay?" said Syrnyk.

"I want my time here to explain my story but I'm not gonna pick up that shotgun and shoot at the cops anymore but I am gonna fuckin' finish this. I will not go to prison. Everything I've done has been totally for being free. I know they can put a fuckin' round through my head from a quarter mile away. But I'm not gonna hurt anybody. I'm not gonna hurt her. I guarantee you." Syrnyk was suddenly concerned about what the operator thought of him. "You know, what I said to you is true. I'm proud of it. I never struck a woman ever because of what I saw. Never struck a child," he said. Johnson asked him to explain what he meant

"What did you see?" she said.

"I'm not assigning any blame, everybody's assigned their own fate. I've come to learn, I live by a code. I'm not ashamed of who I am. There's a lot worse people out there than me. There's fuckin' people that destroy their whole families. They're worse than me." Johnson was trying to interject, to keep Syrnyk's emotions in check, but he wasn't listening to her.

"You don't fuckin' toy with someone's feelings."

"Mike?"

"Is somebody screwing my emotions?"

"Mike?"

"I mean they're gonna find out who I am."

"Mike?"

"In front of God my conscience is clear. I never fuckin' went over the line 'cause I wasn't capable of it. Why do you think all those fuckin' bullets never…"

"Mike? Hello? Mike? Mike!"

"Do you understand that? You know why nobody ever got hit ever, except me? Because that's the way God wanted it and deep down that's the way I wanted it. Now was that not a cool thing?"

"Mike, who's…"

"That was fuckin' miracles over and over and over again."

Johnson was totally confused about what Syrnyk was talking about. "Who hit you?" she asked.

"I got shot that day."

"By who?"

"Oh fuck, you still haven't figured it out, or you're not believing it, but you will find out."

"You know what?" said Johnson. "I do believe you but I don't know who you are and I'm not understanding and I'm not getting a lot of it and I'm sorry for that okay?"

"Well, I mean you must've heard about that asshole that they call the fuckin' Yuletide Bandit?"

CHAPTER 21

Michael Syrnyk had just cut his own throat. Yet he was stunned there wasn't a bigger reaction from the 911 operator, who seemed to be clueless about what he'd just said. Syrnyk had always planned to say it; at least from the moment he had arrived at the massage parlour to confront Megan Ireland. He knew the police would get called. And he was going to be ready to end this nightmare once and for all.

"I got shot at Polo Park. That's me. I mean, don't you read the news or anything? You work at the police station," an incredulous Syrnyk said to the operator. Debbie Johnson was content to simply ask the questions and let Syrnyk keep talking, rather then fill in the blanks herself. "I would've made an amazing detective," he continued. "That's what I wanted to do when I was a kid. I wanted to, but I couldn't stand to be around people 'cause it made me sick to my stomach."

Johnson switched the subject back to Megan, wanting to ensure she was okay. Syrnyk again promised he wasn't going to hurt her. She was free to go, but Syrnyk desperately wanted her to stay when he ended his life. "You don't even have the stomach to watch it, do you?" Syrnyk said to Megan. "I have the stomach to watch it, but it's my own blood." Syrnyk also worried about opening the door to let Megan walk out. "You're gonna get the good old SWAT boys," he told Johnson on the phone. "I'm being straight up here. I'm gonna fuckin' die soon. I'm not going to prison, okay."

Johnson promised Syrnyk that police wouldn't storm the building if he let Megan walk away. "Mike, if you don't want them to come in there, then why don't you walk out, without the gun? You can do it. You can do it," she said.

"And live with a bunch of fuckin' animals? I'm not like those people, okay?"

"If you're not like them you can prove yourself and just walk out," said Johnson.

"Oh yeah, walk out and live in a fuckin' cell for the rest of my life." Syrnyk began to lash out at anyone in power. "I'm actually glad this happened, 'cause you know I did have a lot of bad ideas...I have a hard-on for authority. It's been there all my life. I don't know why. I just hate them and you know what? If a cop can get wounded I'm happy. Is that wrong? I just don't agree with the way things are run."

"Well, a lot of us feel that way as well," said Johnson. She pleaded again with Syrnyk to release Megan. But he refused to go near the door and begged her to stay at his side, still holding both guns in his hands.

"I have gone my whole life without hurting anybody else in any significant way. So why would I fuckin' damn myself now, when I stand in front of God?"

"You know letting her go is not doing anything to yourself," said Johnson. "It's showing that you care about another human being, that's what it would be doing. Okay?"

"You know what? I do care about her. I'm not gonna hurt her," said Syrnyk.

"Then let her go," said Johnson.

"I've lived an interesting life, but most people don't know about it. When it comes right down to the end, the cops gotta admit I was fuckin' smarter than them. I was smarter than those fuckin' pigs. Fuck, I could've been one of them. I would have caught myself by now," Syrnyk continued. Megan could see Syrnyk was completely losing control. She slowly moved towards the door, torn whether she wanted to leave. Syrnyk caught her out of the corner of his eye.

"If you leave, I'm just gonna do it, okay?" Syrnyk said.

"Mike? Why don't you just walk out with her?" said Johnson.

"Why don't I go by the window so you can put a round through my fuckin' head, how about that? They're setting up, aren't they? A nice fuckin' round right in between my fuckin' sternum," he said. Syrnyk's tone suggested a man about to break. "Fuckin' die alone. I'm gonna die here. But you don't have to watch it Meg," Syrnyk said. Megan pleaded with him to change his mind.

"Mike, go with her, okay?" said Johnson.

"No, no I'm not. I'm not going to jail for fuckin' ever, okay," he said. "I want you to stay with me, can you do that? When somebody's dying aren't they at least granted a last wish?" Syrnyk said to Megan.

"I'm staying," she said.

Syrnyk walked away from the phone and snorted another line of cocaine. Megan stayed on the line with the operator, describing his actions. She pleaded with Syrnyk to give her his guns, more for his own safety than hers. Syrnyk got closer to her, and then embraced her in a hug. He was crying. "That's all I wanted, Megan," he said.

"If you want to try and make some promises to him so that he'll walk out there with you, then say anything that you have to, okay," Johnson urged Megan. Megan begged Syrnyk to give her the shotgun and let her put it in another room. Then they would walk out together.

"Listen, just give me the big gun. I don't want you ending up hurting a policeman or whoever," said Megan.

Syrnyk wanted to talk to a police officer, someone involved in major crimes. He wanted it to be a man.

"Obviously, he doesn't get along with women too well anyway," Megan told Johnson.

"Megan, just keep asking him to walk out with you, okay, and just try to get that in his brain," said Johnson.

"I wanna talk to a guy, hello?" Syrnyk interjected.

"There must be somebody around there in charge. I don't think you're fuckin' capable of handling this okay, so get me somebody else. Get a guy, get a detective, or whatever." Johnson was sending messages over her computer terminal, seeking a high-ranking male officer for assistance.

"I'm trying to get someone for you, okay?" she told Syrnyk.

"I'm going away forever. If only there was a death penalty," he said.

Johnson received a speedy reply, saying a crisis negotiator was on his way.

"That's cool. Has he got a brain between his ears?" asked Syrnyk.

"I sure hope so," said Johnson.

Megan was still torn whether to leave. Syrnyk said he wouldn't stop her. "But don't leave me, okay. I'm asking you, I'm not telling you. I just want you to hold my hand just before…" His voice trailed off.

Johnson was anxious for the negotiator to arrive; worried the situation was about to explode in violence. She asked Syrnyk why he'd shot at the two officers.

"'Cause they came to the door with their fuckin' little dicks in their hand," he said.

"Well, you understand they were just trying to do their job, do you?" said Johnson.

"I know, basically they're good guys. But I know why they love their job. They're on a fuckin' power trip," said Syrnyk.

"They just eat on fuckin' people that are basically weaker." Tears began to roll down Syrnyk's cheeks. "I'm not ashamed of anything. I was a thief, and I was a fuckin' good thief. I was just born in the wrong time. Fuck, somebody that needed help when they're a kid and got fuckin' shuffled along, this is what happens. Is this insane the way I'm thinking?"

"No, definitely not," Johnson quickly answered.

"I mean, what was the big harm of me stealing off banks? I'm a thief, I risk my life for money. There's fuckin' honesty in that."

Megan was sitting nearby in a chair, still pondering her fate.

"How the hell did this happen? I mean, don't the cops have this in control at all. They're supposed to know what they're doing. They couldn't catch me, one fuckin' guy," said Syrnyk.

He began rambling on to Johnson about Marlene Griffin and her children, how he could never bring himself to discipline the kids. Johnson could tell the cocaine was getting to him as he drifted between thoughts, often not finishing his sentences. Syrnyk put the phone down again and sat down. One gun remained at his feet while another was in his hand. He was holding the two photographs – one of Marlene, and one of himself as a child. Megan walked over and gave him another hug.

Several minutes passed before Syrnyk returned to the phone.

"What are you doing?" asked Johnson, relieved he was still in a talkative mood.

"Yeah, waiting. Waiting for the white lights. I've seen it a couple times."

Johnson had no idea what he was talking about, but could tell Syrnyk was growing weary. His words were beginning to slur.

"I lived on a street once, and this woman, this Indian woman, was a total crack head drunk. She had twelve kids, and I'd fuckin' come home and there'd be a kid in diapers, two years old, running down the lane. And that kid is fucked. People don't deserve that kind of pain, that kind of ignorance," said Syrnyk. His thoughts were drifting all over the place. "I don't wanna be here, like this is one screwed up fuckin' little planet. I wanna evolve into something else. I'd rather be a tree in the next life." Syrnyk laughed. Johnson did as well.

"But with my luck I'd get cut down and fuckin' turned into cheap furniture."

Sgt. John Ormondroyd arrived in the communications centre, ready to assume command of the delicate situation. He was well-seasoned in hostage and crisis negotiations, ready to take on one of the biggest challenges of his career. Johnson had spent more than 40 minutes on the phone with Syrnyk and was relieved her duties had finished without any bloodshed.

"Hi Mike," Ormondroyd said into the receiver. Syrnyk perked up at the sound of the man's voice.

"This is a movie. A total movie," he said.

• • • • • •

Mark Philippot had never been so happy to see a Winnipeg police uniform. Members of the emergency response unit had secured the three-storey building and stormed the tiny room he was hiding in with the objective of getting him out safely, establishing a perimeter inside the building and containing the suspect. They were fast and efficient. While the man who shot him was tied up on the telephone discussing his fate – and that of his hostage – the ERU quickly moved up to the third floor and hustled Philippot out under heavy guard. It was 90 minutes since Philippot had first entered the downtown complex. The last 88 minutes, spent alone in a tiny drywalled room, felt like an eternity. Emergency dispatchers and radio chatter from fellow officers kept him updated about the situation, but there had been a constant fear the gunman could attempt to ambush him from across the hall. Armed with only his handgun, Philippot worried he would be outgunned. Now, his only concerns were seeing his family, his partner, and getting his own injuries looked at in the hospital.

Diners inside several Chinatown restaurants were finally allowed to leave – under a police escort – following more than an hour of being ordered to stay locked inside. Many were dealt another blow when they walked outside to discover their vehicles were parked inside the police tape. Police had strict orders not to let any cars out of the area, so their night had just gone from bad to worse.

Two ecstasy pills seemed to take the edge off. Syrnyk was actually cracking a few jokes while still holding Megan hostage inside the room. "Is this shit being recorded? I'd like somebody to listen…I guess basically I just always wanted to sing for everybody," Syrnyk told Ormondroyd over the phone line with a chuckle. "Doesn't everybody want me to?" Ormondroyd, like dispatcher Debbie Johnson before him, was being taken on a roller-coaster ride of emotions. Syrnyk wanted to kill himself. Then he didn't. He was remorseful. Then unforgiving. Megan was free to go. But Syrnyk would beg her to stay. It seemed he just wanted to talk.

• • • • • •

Nearly three hours into the ordeal, Syrnyk decided he was finally ready to face his fears alone. He could see Megan was frightened and Syrnyk's anger towards her had greatly subsided during the time they'd spent together in the room. Syrnyk was even regretting bringing her into his mess but believed she had served a useful purpose. "This is the way things were meant to be. You were put here on Earth to help me get caught," Syrnyk told her.

Megan was relieved, albeit somewhat reluctant to leave behind a man she had come to care for, at least on some level. Syrnyk was obviously in serious need of help. But Megan didn't want to die and decided it was time to leave. Syrnyk and Megan had a final, tearful embrace which seemed to last forever. Syrnyk took his guns in hand and backed away as Megan walked towards the door. He worried police officers would storm inside the second she left, and wanted to be ready.

Megan stepped out from the office and was met immediately by the sight of several gun-toting police officers crouched down at the end of the hallway. They shone a blinding light directly in her eyes and screamed for her to put her hands up. Police worried they were walking into a trap. Megan complied, and slowly moved down the hallway towards the light. Syrnyk quickly shut the door behind her, locked it and then tied a piece of rope on the frame for extra security. Police rushed Megan down the stairs and out the front door, directly into a waiting cruiser car. Police had plenty of questions to ask her about her time spent with the mysterious Mr. Syrnyk.

Police officers not tied up at the standoff were being farmed out around the city for additional assistance. Several investigators were dispatched in the late evening hours to 145 Parkview Street, which was the last known address for the man they now knew as Michael Syrnyk. After obtaining a quick search warrant from a magistrate, officers arrived to find the home empty. They took no chances in knocking down the door.

It proved to be a fruitful search. Police found pieces of Kevlar, two Safeway armoured car drop bags, some shotgun shells, garbage bags, a hat and some dark gloves scattered throughout the basement of the home. Some officers were also sent to the Webb Place apartment block where Megan had been living, after she told police Syrnyk had spent some time recently staying in the suite. The search turned up nothing of assistance. Perhaps the biggest discovery came from right under the noses of city police. A 1991 Buick Regal, maroon in colour, was found parked on the street just outside the massage parlour. Police began searching cars in the area once they were able to get Syrnyk's name and checked motor vehicle records registered to him or anyone in his family. The Regal was registered to Syrnyk's father. Inside, officers found a chilling cache of weaponry that made them wonder how much Syrnyk actually had on him, considering what he'd left behind. At least four different guns, including a loaded Remington 12-gauge shotgun, were stuffed inside a duffel bag sitting on the floor of the vehicle. Dozens of triple buck shotgun shells and other ammunition was also scattered in the bag.

It looked like Syrnyk was ready for war.

CHAPTER 22

Winnipeg media gathered en masse outside the standoff scene, with newspaper, television and radio reporters trying their best to make sense out of a situation they knew little about. Two police officers had been grazed by gunfire but had escaped serious injury. A female hostage, believed to be the girlfriend of the gunman, had just been released unharmed. And the mysterious gunman remained holed up inside, his motives and intentions completely unclear.

"He is having a dialogue with us," police spokesman Const. Bob Johnson told reporters on the street at a police command post which was set up about one block west of the standoff. "It's just negotiate, negotiate, negotiate. We're going to be talking to him for some time, trying to get him out of there in a safe fashion. Our negotiations appear to be doing well. He's prepared to talk, which is a good thing."

Johnson told members of the media it was very important to be careful what they reported, because the gunman was likely monitoring the reports and could be influenced by what he sees or hears. Chief Jack Ewatski was also speaking out, having just come from the Health Sciences Centre where he visited both of his wounded officers. "They're both shaken up, and understandably so. But they seem to be in good spirits and doing well considering what happened," said Ewatski.

Smuttell had been extremely worried about Philippot while initially receiving treatment for what was believed to be several shotgun pellets in his shoulder. "When he learned his partner was okay, his spirits lifted," said Ewatski. Several officers, both on and off duty, had gathered in the waiting room at HSC in a show of support for Smuttell and Philippot.

Ewatski's heart sank after receiving the call that two officers were down given the recent climate in Manitoba, in December. Const. Dennis Strongquill, a long-time member of the Royal Canadian Mounted Police, had been ambushed on a darkened highway near Russell – about three hours northwest of Winnipeg – by three fugitives on the run from Alberta, who were now facing charges of first-degree murder. Less than two months later, another Manitoba RCMP officer was shot in the face during routine highway patrols near Portage la Prairie, about an hour west of Winnipeg. The officer, Mike Templeton, managed to survive. Three more Albertans were in custody, charged with attempted murder. The emergency response unit had played a pivotal role in arresting the two suspects, an eight-hour standoff still fresh in their minds. The objective now was the same as it had been on that cold winter night – the safety of officers, protection of the public and to keep the lines of communication open with their suspect. The goal was a peaceful resolution.

• • • • • •

Marvin Simmons had just finished evening services at his Wide World of Faith Church. A ringing telephone greeted Simmons as he entered his home, which was just a short walk down the street from the inner-city parish. It was the Winnipeg police. "Michael Syrnyk wants to talk to you. He says he knows you," the officer said.

Police explained the man was holed up in a nearby office, having already shot two police officers and briefly taken a hostage. He was believed to be high on cocaine and was repeatedly threatening to kill himself. Simmons was perplexed. The name Michael Syrnyk was not familiar, and Simmons didn't understand why this man was specifically asking for him. He wondered if this wasn't one of the many nameless lost souls who pass through his congregation from time to time. Whoever he was, the man clearly needed help.

Simmons kissed his wife good-bye and got into a police cruiser car that came to his home to pick him up and drive him to the scene. Police gave him a quick overview of the situation, telling Simmons the man was very communicative but appeared to be in great distress. Simmons was taken inside the perimeter of the crime scene, where he was given a brief overview of the situation by uniformed officers. He was placed in the backseat of a cruiser car as emergency response unit members reviewed their tactical options inside the command post. For now, Simmons was told to wait. The pastor said he'd do whatever he could to help.

• • • • • •

Alone with his fears, Michael Syrnyk wished Megan Ireland were still at his side. He finished snorting the last of his cocaine and suddenly felt very vulnerable.

The end was near.

Syrnyk's biggest worry was not being able to control his destiny, which he believed would be death. The other option – allowing police to arrest him – was unimaginable. He could never go to prison. Yet despite all his suicidal thoughts, both tonight and in days, months and years past, Syrnyk had been unable to do the deed. He'd felt the cold steel of a gun up against his temple several times already tonight, but was unable to go any further and pull the trigger. The drugs were messing with his mind, preventing him from thinking clearly but also taking his thoughts to the extreme.

Syrnyk could see and hear officers outside the door and knew the building was probably loaded with heavily-armed men clearly looking to avenge what he'd done to the two cops who'd come calling earlier in the night. He took no solace in the promises made by Sgt. Ormondroyd, or the female operator, that

The Yuletide Bandit

police wanted a peaceful resolution. Before he died, Syrnyk wanted to speak to a pastor, to clear his conscience with a man of the cloth. He always felt an unexplainable attraction to the church, and had enjoyed the few services he took in at Marvin Simmons' congregation. While he waited for police to put the pastor on the phone, Syrnyk flipped on a television set located inside the massage parlour. He found a local television newscast and was thrilled to see he was the top story. Syrnyk listened closely to what police said, yelling "bullshit" at the set as they talked about a happy ending. Syrnyk had mixed thoughts when he heard the cops he'd shot were going to be all right. Part of him wished they had died, that he had committed the ultimate act of evil as his final "Fuck You" to the world. Yet the part of Syrnyk, however small, which still housed a heart and a conscience was relieved they would be okay.

Meanwhile, members of the Winnipeg Police major crimes unit couldn't believe what they were hearing. This drugged up psycho in the rub shop, a man named Michael Syrnyk, truly was their Yuletide Bandit? Megan gave a full statement to investigators describing the scar on Syrnyk's leg and his detailed descriptions of some armoured car heists, leaving police shocked but with little doubt. Adding to their certainty were reports coming in from the police communications centre and emergency response unit, which had Syrnyk confessing his involvement in the crime spree they feared they would never crack. It all seemed to good to be true. But who was this man?

Other than the conviction for possessing break-in tools from years ago, Syrnyk's record was spotless. Of all the leads and tips that had poured in over the years, there hadn't been a single mention of this man. It was truly mind boggling, the possibility that a seemingly law-abiding citizen could have done such wrong and managed to conceal it for so long without ever appearing on the radar screen of Winnipeg police. How could they have missed him?

••••••

May 2, 2002

Syrnyk's eyes were becoming heavy, wanting to close, but kept open by a dogged will to remain alert and in control. Police had yet to put Reverend Simmons on the phone, and Syrnyk decided he was tired of negotiating. In fact, he was just plain tired. Three days without sleep and a tidal wave of emotions were finally catching up as Syrnyk sat alone inside the darkened office, contemplating his future. The only light came from a small television set, where Syrnyk had been monitoring Winnipeg television news coverage. Everyone had led with the cop shooting and standoff, and Syrnyk felt a sense of accomplishment that he had everyone talking. He positioned himself on a couch, periodically standing up to glance outside the windows and remind himself of the reality he faced.

Thoughts of suicide would come and go, as did thoughts of Syrnyk's family. He regularly glanced down at the photograph of himself as a child, remembering happier, innocent times when the world wasn't so confusing and messed up. Marlene Griffin's picture also brought a smile to his face. While channel surfing in the early-morning hours, Syrnyk stumbled across a repeat episode of The Simpsons. Syrnyk wasn't fond of sitcoms, but the hit animated show always managed to make him laugh. This night was no different. Syrnyk couldn't help but laugh at tonight's episode. Homer and Marge Simpson, the central married couple in the show, were in the Garden of Eden in a satirical look at creation and religion. Syrnyk was convinced this television show was God's way of speaking directly to him, telling him He was watching over him. Surely this wasn't just a coincidence, not with the deep moral and spiritual conflict Syrnyk had been wrestling with for years.

The good reverend could go home. Police decided against allowing Marvin Simmons to speak directly with their holed-up fugitive, worried it could do more harm than good. Syrnyk was speaking periodically with police, who already had a wealth of information from him and decided it was best not to bring a third party into the conversation. Simmons wasn't about to argue, somewhat relieved he wasn't getting directly involved. Simmons knew there was another way he could help. He would pray for Syrnyk's soul.

• • • • • •

Snow was beginning to gently fall as the early morning temperature dipped unseasonably low. Dozens of police officers, a handful of media and even a few curious citizens who happened to stumble across the police tape and road flares while driving or walking through downtown remained positioned outside as the standoff entered its tenth hour. Intense negotiations were continuing inside the police command centre. Syrnyk's behaviour remained erratic, but police were calm and prepared to play the waiting game. The gunman was only a risk to himself now, and officers wanted desperately to bring him out alive.

At times, Syrnyk appeared almost playful to police – gesturing to officers who he could see positioned outside the office he was holed up in, shouting vulgarities and making faces in an obvious attempt at taunting. Just as quickly as he'd engaged in these silly games, Syrnyk would crash back down to earth by speaking to negotiators in quiet, hushed tones and pondering his place in life and the harm he'd caused to so many people. He was depressed, and even a little scared.

An explosion of glass shattered the relative calm of night. Debris came raining down from the third-floor window, in the office where Syrnyk was hold up. Police prepared for the end, the gunman apparently on a rampage inside. But all that followed was silence.

A completely despondent Syrnyk was ready to stick himself out window he'd just shattered with his feet, put a gun to his head and pull the trigger. Then he would fall gracefully to the ground, landing in the fresh snow that he had been watching fall from the sky for the past hour. It was the kind of scene a Hollywood moviemaker would dream up, and a big part of Syrnyk thought it would be a fitting end to his wasted life. There was just one small problem – Syrnyk couldn't do it.

● ● ● ● ● ●

A thermal imaging camera is one of the best friends of a modern police department. Designed to track body heat and movement through surfaces such as walls, the electronic device can essentially bring police into a hostile environment without physically entering it. Winnipeg police knew they had a hostile environment, but were now wondering if the situation had changed. Syrnyk was no longer visible inside the massage parlour, having apparently moved to another location. More concerning was the fact he was no longer talking to negotiators. Police had lost contact with Syrnyk for quite some time and were now fearing the worst – that he had done as promised and ended his own life. Perhaps it had happened around the time the window got smashed, although police hadn't heard any gunshots. Regardless, it was time for police to re-assess the situation.

Armed with the camera, two members of the emergency response unit began making the tricky climb up the west side of the building housing the massage parlour. Thanks to the fire escape and backup from fellow ERU members, the officers reached the rooftop in mere seconds. Under heavy armed cover they carefully moved along the roof, stopping directly above the room where Syrnyk was holed up. The camera began to do its magic.

● ● ● ● ● ●

The first thing he felt was a leather glove covering his mouth. Another hand followed, this one pinching his nostrils. A stunned Syrnyk awoke from a sleep he hadn't realized he'd taken to the sound of a stampede inside the massage parlour. He struggled for air, writhing around on the couch, unable to escape from the crushing weight against his body. Syrnyk tried to scream, but no sounds came out. He was no longer in control. Finally Syrnyk could fight no more. His mind went blank, his body limp.

Winnipeg police had stormed the room, not wanting to pass up a golden opportunity to literally catch the bandit napping. The thermal camera showed he was alive, but likely asleep. It was precise execution. ERU members quickly contained the two guns that were near Syrnyk's side, located under a jacket that initially gave them some concern because his hands weren't visible. Other officers incapacitated Syrnyk by smothering him out, a common technique that is both safe and successful.

Syrnyk came to with his hands already locked behind his back. It all seemed like a dream. A nightmare really. His worst fears had come true. A man who had spent years in control of his own destiny had gift-wrapped that power and presented it on a platter to Winnipeg police.

The cool night air slapped him in the face as Syrnyk was led out of the building. A few flashbulbs went off in the distance before he was placed in the back of a cruiser car.

This could not be happening.

CHAPTER 23

"I'm glad you guys caught me. This has been eating away at me," a tired, pale-faced Michael Syrnyk told a group of Winnipeg police officers as they sat inside a small interview room at the Public Safety Building. It was just after 8 a.m. – about an hour after he had been arrested. A warm cup of coffee sat in front of him, his hands no longer cuffed. He was slowly coming out of his daze. Police asked Syrnyk, as they are obligated to under the Criminal Code of Canada, if he wished to contact a lawyer. He didn't hesitate in answering no. "What help can I get?" he said rhetorically. Syrnyk didn't want to play any more games, didn't want to hide behind what he'd done. He was going to tell police the whole story, from start to finish. There was no point in trying to hide anymore. The game was over. "No bullshit," Syrnyk promised. He told police they could search his home. The car. His storage locker. The river where he'd dumped the guns. "It looked like I was going to start a war with you guys," he told the officers. Police began to roll the videotape. Syrnyk began to talk.

• • • • • •

May 3, 2002

"You never know what the hell is going on with your neighbours." A Parkview Street resident was holding court with members of the media who had besieged the neighbourhood, looking for every last detail on the Yuletide Bandit. Most residents on this quiet, tree-lined street told the truth – they were completely and utterly shocked. "They were friendly like any other neighbour. I would always talk to them when I see them," said another long-time homeowner. Another described Syrnyk as soft-spoken and easy-going. "He wasn't violent or didn't have a temper of any sort. I guess you really don't know people sometimes," he said.

Winnipeg police wasted no time in throwing the book at Syrnyk and calling for his head.

Only hours after they'd officially laid 62 criminal charges – including the attempted murder of Smuttell and Philippot – police mounted a public relations offensive in demanding the maximum punishment allowed by law. In Canada, that means dangerous offender status. The designation is extremely rare, usually reserved for the most violent and incurable criminals who are deemed to pose a lifetime risk to society. It allows prison officials to keep someone locked up indefinitely, possibly forever. In seven years, a clever and cunning Syrnyk had stolen more than $300,000, damaged more lives than could be counted and led police on a dangerous cat-and-mouse game which everyone managed to survive, if only by the grace of God. "He was very self-disciplined," police Sgt. Doug Lofto said publicly. "But he changed his lifestyle and it caught up with him." Police weren't exactly boasting about finally reeling in the elusive bandit, admitting they caught a lucky break in catching a loose-lipped Syrnyk who willingly led them through his crime spree blow-by-blow. His attention to detail had amazed even the most senior cops, who weren't sure whether to admire Syrnyk or despise him.

Looking tired and worn, a shackled Syrnyk slowly shuffled into courtroom 304 of the downtown Law Courts complex and took a seat in the prisoner's box, flanked by two sheriff's officers. He was very much in a fog, having fallen asleep in the courthouse holding area while waiting for his name to be called for his first court appearance. Syrnyk's dark hair was a tangled mess, large bags visible under both eyes. He started straight ahead as Crown attorney Brian Bell – one of Manitoba's powerhouse prosecutors – addressed the court. "I'm not sure Mr. Syrnyk has contacted a lawyer yet, your honour," Bell told provincial court Judge Judith Webster. The judge asked Syrnyk if this was true.

"No," he mumbled. His case was adjourned until the end of the month.

• • • • • •

A despondent Syrnyk was pacing the floor of his tiny cell inside Headingley Jail. He was a caged animal, trapped in segregation and under 24-hour suicide watch. Having caught up on his sleep, Syrnyk was now very much aware of both his surroundings and his situation. His family – Brent, Sheri, Mike Sr. – were devastated by his arrest. Syrnyk couldn't face the prospect of ever seeing or talking to them again. He was a failure. Time no longer mattered, planning wasn't important. His days and nights were going to be set – filled with nothing but a deep void – for years, if not forever. Syrnyk suddenly exploded with rage, smashing his fist into his face repeatedly, screaming and crying at the same time.

Sporting a black eye, Syrnyk was introduced to his lawyer. Young and energetic, Michael Cook worked for one of the most prestigious law firms in Winnipeg and gladly accepted what would be the biggest case of his career so far. Like most defence lawyers, Cook loved the spotlight and knew a high-profile case was good for business. Cook had no problem ripping off a quick sound bite for the television cameras, walking the fine line so many lawyers do of balancing both his personal and professional interests.

Syrnyk liked Cook from the moment they met, finding his warm smile and positive outlook refreshing. Cook vowed to fight hard for his client, and said the first step would be to get him out on bail. Cook knew it would be a tough battle but felt Syrnyk's strong background and family support would make him the ideal candidate for release. Syrnyk wasn't getting his hopes up, but wasn't going to balk at the opportunity to escape his personal hellhole. Cook began working on a plan he hoped no judge could refuse.

Winnipeg police were developing a new theory about the motives of the Yuletide Bandit. It centred directly on Syrnyk's former lover and close confidant, Marlene Griffin. Marlene was a saint in Syrnyk's eyes, a wonderful woman who could do no wrong. Police weren't wearing the same rose-coloured glasses. Major crime detectives believed Marlene became Syrnyk's primary reason for committing crimes, her constant financial needs driving him deeper into a lifestyle which put dozens of innocent lives at stake. Syrnyk was her lapdog, a devoted puppy that would have stopped at nothing to please the woman he loved.

Both Marlene and Syrnyk adamantly denied their strong bond was based on anything illegal. Syrnyk was especially heartbroken police were dragging Marlene into his mess. He wanted the responsibility to rest entirely on his shoulders and refused to blame his mental health issues, drugs, his parents or anything else for what he'd become.

Police had little evidence to base their theory on, which is why criminal charges against Marlene were only briefly considered before the idea was dropped entirely. Investigators had no doubt she was the one who helped Syrnyk recover after he was shot at Polo Park, and likely was at his side – if not physically, then at least emotionally – during all the subsequent attacks.

But speculation could only get you so far in a court of law.

● ● ● ● ● ●

Bail denied. Provincial court Judge Cathy Everett wasted no time in ordering Syrnyk to remain in custody pending trial. "If these allegations are true, this is a person who is quite literally a ticking time bomb," said a clearly disturbed Everett. Syrnyk was crushed, his pain worsened by the sight of his family in the courtroom. Listening to them read letters of support aloud in court only drove home what a terrible thing he'd done.

Syrnyk was in tears as his brother spoke. "My brother has been deeply lost to an extent that I did not know until now. Despite his actions, he has qualities, which I respect and measure myself against with the hopes of being more like him someday. He is a kind, gentle person with great compassion and understanding. A humour that makes you laugh and think at the same time. A philosopher with a wealth of knowledge, gleaned not just from books, but also from life. I don't know what the future holds for my brother, but I do know that I will be here for him with all my love, support and every ounce of help I can give. I ask that bail be granted, not just for Michael, but also for those of us that love and depend on him. We need him…more than words could possibly say."

Syrnyk's father tendered a bittersweet letter to the court. "I miss my son very much. Michael has created a situation of his own doing and I truly think it has come to an end. If the court, the system, the law is truly interested in recovering Michael from a negative force, to a positive force, the court should consider bail so Michael can be with his family and friends to start this process mentally, before starting his inevitable payment for his actions. I feel Michael is truly someone to be admired for he has released himself from his silent torments in his own flamboyant way. He has truly given of himself again. In closing, I think a brief time with my son is an act God is considering at this moment, for I love my son very much."

Syrnyk's sister-in-law, Sheri, spoke of the strong bond they shared. "Michael has become someone that I depend on and care about deeply. In the last three years, Michael has been there for me on more occasions than I can count. He has taken care of both my animals and myself, numerous times. He even saved the life of one of my dogs. To me, there could not be a kinder, more caring or gentler person than Michael. I ask that bail be considered. If it means anything, I give my word that Michael will be given every bit of support, care and guidance that his friends and family can possibly give. Now that we are aware of his problems, we can help him on the road to recovery. I also ask that bail be given to Michael to tie up loose ends. His mother recently passed away, and not being able to visit the cemetery to say his peace would be a very heavy burden."

Syrnyk's heart felt like it was ripped from his chest as he read the contents of Marlene's handwritten letter. "I feel it is important for people to know the kind of person Michael is, and what importance and impact he has on my life and those of my three children. Mike has always been a very caring, loving and gentle person around my children and me. They grew very close in a short period of time, and Mike was very attentive and playful at all times with them. He was more caring and attentive than their own father. Right now my children are very confused as to what has happened to him, and they ask about him all the time, they miss him greatly and want to see him again. Michael is not anything like most criminals. I am asking that he be granted bail, even for a short period of time, under whatever restrictions may be imposed, for myself as someone who loves him very much, and for my children who see him more like a father than their own. We ask for a period of time to spend with Michael to resolve ourselves to the incarceration period he faces and to have a few special moments to lessen the pain of him being ripped from our lives."

Cook had tried his hardest, offering up a $20,000 surety that Syrnyk's family was prepared to pool together. If Syrnyk breached his bail, the money was gone. Syrnyk would also have been under a 24-hour daily curfew. Everett was moved by the show of support, which included more than a dozen glowing letters in total. Everyone described him as a model citizen and all-around wonderful human being, the type of young man every mother would love their daughter to bring home. A former neighbour described how Syrnyk helped him out when he was felled by a stroke by doing some shopping for him. Another told court how Syrnyk always helped shovel his snow or collect his mail when he was out of town. Others spoke of his devotion to his dying mother. And his interest in the church.

"What I have before me is a plan put forward by a very loving family who want the best for him," said Everett, who couldn't justify freeing someone who had confessed to terrorizing so many people for so long. A despondent Syrnyk took one last glance at his family through his teary eyes before he was taken out of the courtroom and back to the hellhole that was now his home.

The kind words of his loved ones were echoing inside Syrnyk's head. He couldn't stop seeing their disappointed faces. Syrnyk couldn't take it any longer. He knew it was finally time. There would be no more wavering.

Holding a razor he'd grabbed from the shower area, Syrnyk held it up to the right side of his throat. There was no fear. Just anticipation. The blade cut easily through his flesh, and Syrnyk felt the warm flow of blood on his neck. He began flexing his neck muscles, trying to increase the bloodletting.

Syrnyk was feeling extreme peace as he began to lose consciousness.

• • • • • •

One centimetre. Syrnyk had come so very close to ending his life, just missing a major artery. Now, he was back in protective custody, on intense suicide watch, bearing an ugly red scar on the left side of his throat as a permanent reminder of his failure. Life couldn't get any worse. Two Winnipeg police investigators came to see him shortly after his failed attempt. "I've been really out to lunch. I don't even know this person anymore," Syrnyk told them. "This person is dead."

• • • • • •

June 20, 2002

With his family sitting glumly in court, a pale-faced Rene Sylvestre apologized for his minor role in the one of the worst armed robbery rampages in Manitoba history. Rene pleaded guilty to helping Syrnyk with the in-your-face S.I.R. Warehouse robbery in March only weeks after police charged him. "I just want to say I'm sorry to the victims. I've had a lot of guilt since my arrest," Rene said in his thick French accent. His parents, grandfather, brother, sister and uncle all sat quietly in the public gallery. Rene's lawyer, Brad King, played up the impact of cocaine on his young client, saying it drove him to desperate measures. The chance meeting with Syrnyk was a recipe for disaster. King and Crown attorney Brian Bell agreed the minimum sentence – four years in prison – was proper for Rene, who had no prior criminal record. In Canada, robbery with a firearm carries the mandatory minimum of four years. Police and the Crown suspected Rene might have been involved in some of Syrnyk's other crimes but didn't have any evidence to proceed with additional charges. Rene promised to work hard at turning his life around, gave his supportive family a weak smile and was led out of the courtroom in handcuffs to begin serving his punishment.

● ● ● ● ● ●

Club 205 was out of business. The infamous Winnipeg massage parlour lost its municipal operating licence amid the public and political fallout that came with playing host to a violent hostage taking and standoff. Rev. Harry Lehotsky, an inner-city activist who runs the New Life Ministries Church, was among the parlour's many vocal critics. "I can't imagine anyone in their right mind would say a massage parlour is good for the revitalization of the inner city," he told city representatives. A two-member appeals committee agreed, stripping the club of its licence. Ken Wong, a well-known businessman in Winnipeg's Chinese community who owns the entire building, tried to argue the economic hardship he would face if he lost his tenant would be crippling. Vic Savino, the lawyer for the massage parlour, argued the high-profile crime was an isolated event.

"This business is a legal operation with no connection to organized crime. We're not here to legislate morality, we're here to see if a licence should be granted." His pleas fell on deaf ears.

••••••

Rick Long was back at the McPhillips Street Safeway for the first time in nearly three months. His body tensed up as he approached the parking lot while seated inside his armoured car. Long had just returned to work on a part-time basis while still under the care of a psychologist. A chalk mark was still visible on an outside pillar as Long walked in the front door of Safeway. A chill shot through him – it was the police outline of one of the bullets he had ducked.

Long gathered his composure and pressed on, picking up a large bag of coins and returning to his truck. His partner was still inside when something caught the corner of his eye. A person, seemingly coming out of nowhere, was headed his way in a hurry. Long jumped, reaching instinctively for his gun.

False alarm.

A hurried customer, seemingly oblivious to his prescience, was just taking a short cut to the store's front entrance by cutting between the truck and the doors. Long needed another cigarette.

It wasn't long before he was in the news again. Long, still seething at being victimized, told Winnipeg media outlets the public doesn't fully appreciate what he and his colleagues went through.

"We were outside a North End credit union the other day and some guy comes at me with his arms out, like he's pretending he's going to shoot. It was stupid, stupid, stupid," Long said in an interview. "People seem to have such a short memory. I'll be walking with the money and someone will cut between my partner and me. They should not do that. They should just stay away from us so we can do our job and leave."

Long said he'd come to realize God was watching over him that fateful day.

"We fired 14 rounds in a busy public place. It's a miracle nobody was killed. A couple of people have told me I had two angels sitting on my shoulders that day. Two of his bullets missed me by inches," he said. "It just wasn't my time on that day. Or his, apparently."

● ● ● ● ● ●

July 5, 2002

Michael Syrnyk was not your typical criminal. Dr. Kent Somers, a registered psychologist who has worked with some of the sickest, most twisted felons in Manitoba, knew he was dealing with someone quite unique. Assigned by the courts to paint a picture of Syrnyk's mind, Somers met four times with his reluctant subject in the past two weeks. Syrnyk amazed him with his display of intellect. But Somers could also see a deeply troubled man who was clearly demoralized, defeated and quite miserable. Somers administered a series of tests exploring Syrnyk's language abilities, reading skills and cognitive and emotional behaviour. "His score on the vocabulary subtest suggests Mr. Syrnyk likely has oral language skills that are commensurate with, or perhaps somewhat stronger than those of the average adult his age," Somers wrote in his report. Ditto for Syrnyk's prowess on comprehension of common social norms and conventions.

Syrnyk's only problem was with a test to measure short-term memory, which was quite weak. Somers attributed it to several factors, including stress and a chronic history of anxiety. Syrnyk also aced reading comprehension tests, but fell apart when it came time to study his emotions. Somers wrote: "Mr. Syrnyk presents as having longstanding difficulties in relating to others and managing his thoughts and emotions. He is unlikely to have internally cohesive means of coping with difficulties in life; his moods are likely to be enigmatic and his behaviours contradictory. He may behave in ways that are self-defeating: for example, in wanting social approval and support, but expecting none, he may shun or withdraw from others, precluding support. He may interpret this action as corresponding to others' disapproval, and thus to feel humiliated, despondent and unworthy. His isolation insulates an anxious depression, which then finds expression indirectly, in petulance or passive aggressive acts. His propensity for depression likely results in chronic dysphoria, dissatisfaction with his life, a deep sense of self-loathing and feelings of exhaustion and apathy."

The Yuletide Bandit

"Clinically, Mr. Syrnyk presents as a depressed individual. Self-pity, feelings of emptiness and apprehension, feelings of guilt, thoughts of death, distractibility, fatigue and diffuse anxiety are all consistent with this presentation. His responses suggest the possibility that Mr. Syrnyk has experienced a psychotic episode, that is, a period of regressive behaviour and shutting down of emotional resources. Bizarre ideation, behavioural withdrawal and emotional blunting may occur, or be allowed to occur as a means of disqualifying logic and evading responsibility. Retreat into these distorted patterns of relating to others and to the difficulties in his life may have prevented Mr. Syrnyk from experiencing genuine feelings associated with perceived loss and failure of rejection."

In other words, Syrnyk was a giant head case. Somers suggested major intervention to deal with Syrnyk's "social isolation" and the dependence he developed on drugs and alcohol as a dangerous means of self-medicating. Somers blamed much of Syrnyk's problems on family violence issues that he believes led to mental health issues that quickly raged out of control. His diagnosis was limited because Syrnyk was reluctant to discuss his family background in any detail. Somers found Syrnyk was likely more of a risk to himself than to regular citizens. His social and emotional issues that led him to crime now threatened to completely destroy him.

"He was candid in reporting about his criminal career. He reported that crime served a number of functions. It provided him with the financial means to live given that he found conventional work, and dealing with the public, to be intolerable. It provided him with sufficient income that he could indulge in the frequenting of massage parlours. Crime also provided him with sufficient income to indulge his substance abuse, which served, beyond its immediate pleasure, to relieve his reported symptoms of depression and anxiety," wrote Somers. "Finally, offending provided him with concrete proof of his power, efficacy, and accomplishment in the world in contrast to his typical feelings of powerlessness, fear, futility and failure. These robberies allowed him to face down his fears and conquer them in a dramatic, immediate and undeniable manner. Fear was replaced by elation."

Syrnyk had been reluctant at first to speak with the doctor, but felt better after the four meetings at Headingley Jail. At times, it was as if Syrnyk was speaking about two completely different people when he described his life to the doctor. Thoughts of death had waned in recent days as Syrnyk became more settled in his environment and began taking stock of his life, including people who still cared for him deeply. In many ways, he was proud of what he'd done, how successful he'd been. But he also wished there was some way to turn back the clock, back to the innocent little boy in the photograph he clutched so tightly in his hands the night of the stand-off. Syrnyk didn't want to waste any more time, and instructed his lawyer to get him into court to deal with his charges as soon as possible. There was no sense putting off the inevitable.

CHAPTER 24

December 17, 2002

The day of reckoning had arrived. Seven months since Michael Syrnyk's arrest, the courts were finally ready for him. Syrnyk wanted to do it much sooner but had been delayed while his lawyer reviewed boxes of evidence forwarded by police and the prosecution. The passage of time, however, had given Syrnyk the chance to stabilize his emotions. His family was visiting and speaking with him regularly, desperately trying to convince Syrnyk he had plenty to live for. The message had started getting through. Thoughts of suicide had largely subsided and Syrnyk was allowed to return to the general population. He still loathed the environment and found the days excruciatingly long as he mainly kept to himself and completely avoided any trouble. Syrnyk was a loner behind bars, just as he had been in the outside world for so many years.

Rick Long wanted a front-row seat. He needed to be able to look the man who forever changed his life directly in the eyes, to put a real human face to the horror. Only this time, the man couldn't hide behind a mask. An emotional Long walked into the courtroom, the only civilian victim to accept the Crown's invitation to attend the hearing. He wished he could speak directly to the bandit, to ask him what the hell he was thinking. Long would never understand. He quietly took a seat near Daryl Smuttell and Mark Philippot, the two wounded police officers who also wanted to face their attacker. A door leading into the prisoner's box began to open. The shackled man walked in flanked by two sheriff's officers. Long didn't blink.

Mike Syrnyk Sr., his son Brent and daughter-in-law Sheri felt a tug of their hearts as a scrawny, dejected Syrnyk slumped in the prisoner's box. They wanted desperately to go to him, to remind him they were here for him. Instead, they sat in silence. Syrnyk knew his family had ignored his pleas to stay away from court. Now he struggled to turn his eyes towards the public gallery. He didn't want anyone to see the fear in his eyes, or the pain. It was easier just to look down. It had always been easier that way.

Manitoba's justice department wanted life in prison. Stopping just short of asking for dangerous offender status, Crown attorney Brian Bell said anything short of the maximum prison term would be an insult to the dozens of victims Syrnyk terrorized over the years. He requested parole eligibility be raised from the normal seven years to 10.

The Yuletide Bandit

"Mr. Syrnyk is a very dangerous man," Bell said in his opening remarks.

Syrnyk's anger towards society, his extreme planning and pre-meditation of his crimes and the length of his crime spree couldn't be ignored. One by one, the charges were read aloud in court. In total, Syrnyk was forced to mumble "guilty" 35 different times, which included 15 armed robberies, nine armoured-car heists and the shootings of two city police officers. As hard as it was to fathom, it could have been worse.

The Crown didn't even bother to lay stolen car charges that likely would be in the hundreds, figuring they would simply get lost in the bigger picture. Bell also dropped 33 other charges that stemmed out of the same incidents and were mainly a result of over-charging by police. A charge of wearing a disguise is somewhat moot when Syrnyk was already admitting to the robbery with a firearm offence. Bell spent the entire day pouring through the facts in painful detail that left Syrnyk squirming in his seat. He credited Syrnyk with bringing to light many crimes which would likely have gone unsolved if not for his admissions to police. "He has been quite candid with his involvement," said Bell. Statements from tearful victims and stunned witnesses were read aloud in court, as Syrnyk sat with his head bowed, playing each crime over in his head.

Bell closed his submission with a bang, tendering a victim impact statement from Smuttell, the wounded cop.

"The emotional impact of the shooting has affected my feelings, reactions and ability to work. I do find that I am easily startled by loud, sudden noises. Example – a door being slammed hard or something hitting the floor making a bang. In relation to my ability to work, I find that some situations at work now bother me or stress me in ways that did not before the shooting. I find that I am apprehensive at work entering some situations and I hope that never will put myself, my partner or the public in danger should I hesitate during a situation," Smuttell wrote. "My family, friends and colleagues have been very supportive throughout the incident, however, I do find the need for some reason to be alone more often than before the shooting, as not a day goes by that I don't think about the images of that day. I was very lucky I was surrounded by three co-workers who I had a very good relationship with and confidence in."

Smuttell detailed his physical recovery, which included hospitalization for a day, several weeks of pain medications, two weeks of homecare, ongoing counselling through the police staff psychologist and too many sleepless nights to count. But the most chilling reminder was a single pellet still lodged in his arm, directly against the bone. Doctors feared it would cause more harm than good in trying to remove it. Smuttell also bears two permanent scars on his left arm from pellets that entered his body.

"I was very lucky to be alive after being shot. This crime could probably not happen two times in a row without it being fatal," said Smuttell.

* * * * * *

December 18, 2002

Now it was Syrnyk's turn to talk. Only there was nothing that really could be said to justify what he'd done. Defence lawyer Mike Cook had the monumental task of following up the Crown's damning submission with one that could persuade the judge to give Syrnyk something less than the maximum. Cook focused on the report by Dr. Somers that showed Syrnyk's lifetime battle with depression and anxiety. Cook also noted his client's deep remorse, illustrated through his co-operation with police and desire to plead guilty and spare all the victims from the pain of testifying. A thick stack of reference letters, penned by Syrnyk's family members and close friends of the family, spoke volumes of the man seated in the prisoner's box and his prospects for rehabilitation. "The Michael that went into incarceration seven months ago is not the Michael of today. He is incredibly remorseful for his actions. He has spent every day wishing he could take back the last eight years of his life, take back all the pain he has caused by his thoughtless actions," wrote Syrnyk's sister-in-law, Sheri. "Michael is honestly thankful he was apprehended. It allowed him to stop what he could not stop on his own. He now sees that he has another chance at life, a chance to have a good life with the love and support of those he believed could not help him before. I am aware that Michael must seem like a monster to you. He isn't."

Brent poured his heart out in a letter to the court. "Needless to say, none of our lives will quite be the same from this day forth. I am painfully aware of what lies ahead for someone I admire and have depended on for as long as I can remember. Since Mike was incarcerated in May, I have been going to visit him every Saturday afternoon. I look forward to these visits all week, and I know Mike does too (there is always a mad dash for the phone in our house, in hopes it will be Mike). These conversations are often lengthy and revolve around Mike's regrets of the past and the many wrong turns he has taken. He refers to himself in the past and says the person he was is now 'dead'," Brent wrote. "Just a few weeks after Mike was arrested, I had the sad experience of going through and cleaning up some of his personal stuff. In amongst scraps of paper and books, I found a receipt made out to the Children's Wish Foundation in the amount of $1,000. This receipt was made out in the name of one of Mike's favourite movie characters. Knowing the goodness my brother has in him, this did not surprise me one bit."

Syrnyk managed a weak smile at the reference, remembering vividly the day he decided to use some of his stolen cash for good, rather than just feeding his own addictions to sex and drugs. It was a rare bright spot in an otherwise bleak existence.

"The last seven months away from him has left me with an understanding of what he means to me, and how incredibly painful and empty the days have been without him...and will be to come," Brent concluded.

Cook made a final plea with the judge to give Syrnyk some hope, a light at the end of the tunnel. He suggested 15 years in prison was more than enough punishment. Provincial court Judge Charles Newcombe was clearly torn. He wondered aloud how he could give anything less than life without making many of Syrnyk's crimes "freebies" and catering to a "cheaper by the dozen" philosophy of sentencing. "What does that say to the major, or minor, villains on the street who remain at large? You've got two or three crimes under you already, so you might as well walk into a bank and commit more offences because they're freebies?" asked the judge.

Newcombe needed a few days to sleep on the decision, but didn't want to wait too long to pass sentence. With the holiday season looming, Newcombe, Bell and Cook consulted their diaries and came up with their only available date for his decision on the fate of the Yuletide Bandit. Christmas Eve.

● ● ● ● ● ●

December 24, 2002

Winnipeg shoppers no longer had to worry about a gun-toting madman ruining their holidays – and possibly ending their lives – by making his ugly mark on Christmas. While most people made final holiday preparations, Michael Syrnyk was spending his morning waiting for a judge to decide his future. Judge Newcombe walked into the courtroom right at 9 a.m., sternly told everyone in the gallery to sit down and wasted no time in getting down to business.

"Mr. Syrnyk was prepared to risk the lives of man, woman, child, the infirm, the elderly alike, whether it was being struck by a bullet, buckshot round, directly or by ricochet, crushed in a panic, or run down by fleeing motorists," Newcombe began. "He progressed from a nervous, bungling amateur to a rather cunning professional. It is fair to say that Mr. Syrnyk was a very real threat to the community generally, to say nothing of tellers, messengers and guards. It is equally fair to say that such wanton egregiously reckless criminality must be deterred." Newcombe focused for a few moments on the letters of support for Syrnyk. "All describe a shy, lonely man who was, to them at least, gentle, loyal and considerate. Their opinions describe a man who possesses qualities in keeping with the realistic hopes of his eventual rehabilitation. Those who know him most intimately agree up on his longstanding need for professional, psychological or psychiatric intervention. I accept their opinions as honest and fair. What undercuts their weight to some degree is the complete lack of appreciation these friends, neighbours, father and brother had for the man that Mr. Syrnyk became while outside their immediate company," said the judge. "It is Mr.

The Yuletide Bandit

Syrnyk's misfortune that his careful planning, his cunning and his good luck in escaping both crime scenes and a debilitating wound permitted his depredations to span eight years and many, many, many acts of violence. A court is left with very little room to manoeuvre in ameliorating what by the standards of this jurisdiction will be a very heavy sentence for crimes that do not include homicides. One can only hope that his confession to many of these offences which the Crown likely could not have otherwise proved is evidence of remorse and atonement rather than self-aggrandizement."

Twenty-three years. Newcombe had stopped short of life, but also gone far beyond the defence recommendation. He broke the sentence down by giving 17 years for all the robberies, and six years consecutive for the police shootings. Newcombe wanted the punishment for those crimes to stand out from the rest.

"Police officers choose a career in which they serve as protectors of society from those such as Mr. Syrnyk. They risk injury and worse to stand between ourselves and criminals. As they are duty bound to protect us in a physical sense, so we are obligated as a society to protect and support them," he said.

"There exists an unwritten but binding social contract that society's obligation is manifested in part by its responsibility through its courts to denounce and deter by way of penal sanction those who cause harm to our protectors. The Syrnyks of this world are relatively rare, yet he is neither the first nor the last criminal who, facing substantial periods of incarceration, will consider the use of deadly force to avoid arrest."

Syrnyk sat stone-faced as he listened to the decision, the judge's voice becoming mere background noise as the numbers floated through his head. How could he ever last? Even with parole, he would still have to do nearly eight years before he was eligible. He turned to his family in the gallery, who looked shattered as he was led out of the courtroom for a final time. Syrnyk had to turn away, disgusted with himself.

• • • • • •

The kudos were rolling in for Winnipeg police. Debbie Johnson, the operator who kept the Yuletide Bandit talking on the phone during the first hour of the Chinatown stand-off, was given the 2003 Association of Public Safety Communication Canada public safety communicator award. The national award credited Johnson with keeping her cool and helping to prevent what could have been a massacre. "I was just doing my job," a modest Johnson said at a police news conference. "I just wanted to get everyone out okay. We take tough calls all the time. You treat it as one call at a time."

Police Insp. Shelly Hart wasn't as modest as Johnson. "This was just about as challenging as calls come," said Hart. She said Johnson's award is a morale boost to the entire police service, which had come under fire in 2000 for its handling of several 911 calls placed by two sisters who were eventually murdered. An inquest into that case had recommended sweeping changes to the 911 system.

Meanwhile, the two police officers shot and wounded on the job were also recognized for their bravery. Smuttell and Philippot were given the Canadian Professional Police Association awards of excellence at an August 2003 ceremony in Edmonton.

● ● ● ● ● ●

Staff from the Salvation Army visit Stony Mountain penitentiary every Monday morning, offering religious services for inmates desperately in need of some personal cleansing. Some are there simply because finding God seems to be the chic thing to do while in prison, a quick and easy way to wipe their conscience clean and hopefully score some points in court. Others attend for deeper, more spiritual reasons. They truly are lost souls in need of guidance. Michael Syrnyk still doesn't know why he attends.

"I'm still not sure if I believe in God. It has yet to be proven. My thoughts are overwhelming at times, and I can never come to any concrete decision," Syrnyk says to a visitor inside an interview room in late February 2004. The wind is howling outside, as winter takes what many hope is a parting shot at Manitoba.

"I often wonder if I wasn't meant to be involved with religion. In many ways, it played a big part in my crime spree, especially at the end."

Syrnyk continues speaking, taking long pauses between sentences. "You know, I'm afraid of how emotionless I'm becoming. This place is scary. Prison just numbs you, to the point you don't feel anything."

Syrnyk has lost nearly 25 pounds since his sentencing and it shows in his gaunt face. He sucks on a cough drop and stares at the triangle tattoos on his bony arms. His hands are trembling.

Syrnyk is sickened by what he is seeing in prison. Rapists and murderers who openly brag about their crimes. A prison pecking order where the strong eat the weak. And street gangs running amuck. Syrnyk felt physically sick recently when an episode of the hit television show "The Sopranos" was playing in prison. Inmates gathered around the television laughed with glee at a horrific scene where a man is killed execution-style. The room began spinning for Syrnyk; not unlike the feeling he had as a teenager trying to board a transit bus.

Syrnyk tries to avoid contact with fellow inmates wherever possible. He spends much of his time reading books, working odd jobs in the prison and talking to loved ones on the telephone. Guards describe him as a model inmate who keeps to himself and is always polite. Syrnyk is back to speaking regularly with Marlene Griffin and her children after months of being unable to even dial her number. But he draws the line at visiting – Syrnyk has refused to let them come and see him in prison, keeping their conversations strictly by telephone. Tears well up in his eyes as he speaks about the children who had accepted him in their lives as their father. His failure overwhelms him. "I just can't handle it at times," he says.

Syrnyk recently received a letter from Megan Ireland, who has now moved to Alberta. They have not seen each other since he let her go inside the massage parlour. Thoughts of their brief time together are mostly positive for Syrnyk, who believes it was fate for them to meet and provide a means for him to end his madness. "This all kinda feels like a movie," she told the *Free Press* during an interview in 2002. "It's like we got involved in this on-going, whacked out, metaphysical conversation all for his benefit. It's like I was put in this place to help him get caught."

If there is one reason for hope in Syrnyk's life, it comes in the form of a baby girl. Born to his brother and sister-in-law in late 2003, the child is never far from his thoughts. Syrnyk calls Brent and Sheri daily, just to check up on his family. He wants to make sure they're doing okay.

Brent, Sheri and the baby visit every Sunday morning, the few hours spent together providing Syrnyk enough strength to last another week. There are good days and bad days for Syrnyk, where thoughts of harming himself creep back into his mind. He quickly talks himself down from the emotional ledge. "I'd rather just be taken out and shot, just to see how I could face it. All I know is, this way of living is disgusting," Syrnyk says. But Syrnyk is adamant he wants to live, if not for himself then for the people who clearly do care about him and want him to remain in their lives. They were always there. Only now Syrnyk can finally see them.

He has a handle on his emotional distress, relying on anti-depressant medication to control his chemical imbalances. The Monday morning church services are medicine for his mind; a spiritual awakening that allows Syrnyk to dream about a future. But his past threatens to always get in the way.

"I wasn't out to destroy innocent people," Syrnyk insists. "We're all out to feel powerful. That's what this was all about."

"Before I began this rampage, I truly believed life was meaningless. To me, everything was a reflection of lies, bleak and tainted. I lost faith in the human condition because I lacked the skills to acquire contentment in my own life. Confused by envy, hating myself, the pain I felt somehow became a licence to lash out at society. I rejected rational thought and became a tyrant drained of ordinary morality. I lived in my own world and there the rules did not apply to me. Vice and avarice fuelled a disturbed lifestyle. Narcotics wiped my thoughts and dulled my conscience. As my dangerous and violent behaviour escalated, I found myself suicidal and losing my grasp on reality. These conditions, present from the beginning, only intensified over time. I was so far gone. For me there was no deterrent in the absence of any belief system. I was consistently rewarded for my efforts.

Now it is with a nightmarish quality that I replay my former life and accept punishment as the only way I was ever going to learn the truth. Basically I became an expert in lying to myself and took the easy way out in all things. The truth is I couldn't hack it in the real world. After only a short period of reflection and countless realizations I now *find myself tormented by what I became. Of my actions I experience humiliation and self disgust on a daily basis. It is only necessary that I have come to this time and place. In the end no one ever escapes justice or themselves. The all too real feeling that I was in grave danger of losing so much more than just my freedom or my life. In my estimation an apology to my innocent victims would seem hypocritical. I've hurt so many people and for that I'm getting what I deserve. I know people hate me and it's justified. I can only imagine the depths of contempt certain parties hold for me, the guards directly and indirectly involved and their families. I know I've done great damage to the lives of Constable Smuttell and Constable Philippot. If it's any consolation, I am suffering under my present situation, the reality of a wasted life and falling so far from who I once was. If the terrifying lack of control I now feel for my own life is in any way comparable to how I impacted the lives of my victims, then I have finally come to realize the horrible nature of my crimes. I can't express in words the shame and remorse I feel for such a public display of ignorance and wrath. In the future I need to embrace rehabilitation through education in order to one day earn the stability in life that has eluded me for so long.*

Ultimately, I am thankful it's over. Without a mask to hide behind, I can see myself through your eyes. I hate what I see and I have to face myself every day. I thought my moment of truth would come with a bullet. I never believed I ever would have to face you. I suppose confession is good for whatever I have left. By my own free will I became the worst human being I could imagine, all because of one fatal flaw.

The Yuletide Bandit

For as long as I can remember, to me, asking for help from others I considered disgusting and shameful. Alone too long with my own thoughts, I have no one to blame but myself."

– **Michael Syrnyk**